Honeypots and Routers

Collecting Internet Attacks

Honeypots and Routers

Collecting Internet Attacks

Mohssen Mohammed · Habib-ur Rehman

CRC Press
Taylor & Francis Group
Boca Raton London New York

CRC Press is an imprint of the
Taylor & Francis Group, an **informa** business
AN AUERBACH BOOK

CRC Press
Taylor & Francis Group
6000 Broken Sound Parkway NW, Suite 300
Boca Raton, FL 33487-2742

First issued in paperback 2020

© 2016 by Taylor & Francis Group, LLC
CRC Press is an imprint of Taylor & Francis Group, an Informa business

No claim to original U.S. Government works

ISBN-13: 978-1-4987-0219-5 (hbk)
ISBN-13: 978-0-367-65867-0 (pbk)

Visit the Taylor & Francis Web site at
http://www.taylorandfrancis.com

and the CRC Press Web site at
http://www.crcpress.com

Contents

1

COMPUTER NETWORKS

HABIB-UR REHMAN

A computer network typically comprises three components: devices, medium, and topology. Computers, smartphones, laptops, routers, switches, and repeaters are the different kinds of devices that may exist in a computer network. In order to communicate with each other, these devices are connected by a medium, either wireless or wired. The resulting schematic of the devices linked through the medium is the topology of the network.

In a computer network, communication actually happens among devices. In the context of human conversations, the term *communication* encompasses a complete dialog between two persons. The same rule applies to computer networks: communication among two or more devices may consist of more than one message exchanged among the participating devices. *Session* is a more widely used technical term to describe a series of correlated messages exchanged among devices.

Before we move further into our discussion of computer networks, let us recall the example of postal service commonly described in the textbooks to explain how a computer network functions. A house may have more than one resident, who can be a sender or receiver of messages. All these residents share the same address; however, the actual sender/recipient is identified by the name mentioned on the envelope. The postal service is usually neither the sender nor the recipient but the messages pass through it, and it facilitates the transmission of messages. The recipient address is used to deliver the message to its destination and the source address is used to identify its originator. The message itself is usually some data or information arranged in a comprehensible way for the recipient. The overall assembly of the message should also be comprehensible for the postal service, so that the sender and recipient addresses are distinguishable, identifiable, and locatable.

When computers communicate, constraints such as being comprehensible, distinguishable, or identifiable require precise and comprehensive establishment of the procedures and regulations for the delivery of message(s). This brings the fourth component of computer networks into the picture: the protocol. Protocols and standards are the set of rules and procedures followed by the devices during communication.

This chapter is divided into four sections, each reviewing one of the four components of the computer network.

1.1 Devices

A device typically plays one of the three roles in a message exchange: it originates a message, or it is the recipient of the message, or the message passes through it. The device initiating a message is usually called *source* or *origin*, while the recipient(s) of a message is (are) called *destination(s)* or *sink(s)*. Together the two are called *end nodes* or *end devices*. When the two end devices are not connected directly, the message passes through one or more intermediate devices. The end devices are generally the computing devices used by the end users such as PCs, phones, and tablets (tabs); on the other hand, the intermediate devices are usually special-purpose devices with the objective of facilitating the transmission between the end devices.

Based on its role in the communication, a device has to perform several steps in a particular order to make the communication successful. For example, the job of the source device is to specify the address of only the destination device and not that of the destination or intermediate devices. The open systems interconnection (OSI) reference model, as it is usually called, is a conceptual description of the tasks and duties performed by devices while communicating in a computer network. This abstract model divides the activities, based on their relevance and dependency, into seven groups referred to as *layers*: physical, data link, network, transport, session, presentation, and application (Figure 1.1).

The primary purpose of a computer communication is to facilitate the users and deliver the data or information. The user interacts with the computer system, the device of our communication scenario, through some application; the data or information provided to the system or received from the system is usually in a user comprehensible format. Due to this fact, the end devices generally perform all the

7	Application
6	Presentation
5	Session
4	Transport
3	Network
2	Data link
1	Physical

Figure 1.1 ISO/OSI reference model for network communication.

actions described in the OSI model, or in other words, implement all the seven layers. The intermediate nodes, on the other hand, might be implementing a limited number of layers (or performing tasks related to fewer layers) according to their role in the communication. One way to categorize the devices in a computer network is to group them according to the layer they belong.*

As mentioned earlier, the user mostly interacts with the end devices, which are typical computing devices. However, the communication always involves multiple intermediate devices sitting in the core of the network joining the two ends. Next, we mention the four important categories of intermediate devices commonly participating in a computer communication.

1.1.1 Modem

The job of a modem is to convert digital signals to analog signals and vice versa. Modems are generally required when devices perform digital communication over the telephone network. By definition, a modem performs *mo*dulation and *dem*odulation only, a task that belongs to OSI layer 1. However, in almost all the cases, the functionality of the appropriate layer 2 is part of the device.

---

* The presence of the functionality of an upper OSI layer in a device requires that it should perform the tasks of all the lower layers as well, that is, it should implement all the layers up to that level. Hence, if we say a device is a layer 3 device or belongs to layer 3, this means that it implements (or performs the actions associated with) all the layers from layer 1 to layer 3.

1.1.2 Bridge

A bridge is a device that operates at layer 2 of the OSI reference model and connects two smaller networks together into one, so that the devices in the two segments can communicate with each other. The devices are connected to the bridge through its ports individually in most of the cases. However, multiple bridges can also be joined through the same ports when more than two smaller networks are combined. Bridges are commonly referred to as *switches*, although, the term *switch* has broader technical meanings. Further details of the functionality of the bridges are mentioned in Section 1.4.1.

1.1.3 Router

Routers are also devices that combine one or more networks into one; however, they belong to layer 3 of the OSI model. This implies that routers perform more and complicated tasks as compared to bridges. Typically, unlike bridges, the devices are not directly connected to the ports of the router; it is in fact the bridges that are connected to the routers. Multiple routers can also be connected to each other to combine the networks attached to each of them. The operations and characteristics of the routers are also described later in Section 1.4.2.

1.1.4 Gateway

Imagine a student in China who wants to send his admission request to a university in Canada by postal service. What happens if he writes the recipient address only in the Chinese language; how would the postal staff in Canada deliver it? When two networks following different communication protocols or standards are joined together, a network device is required to perform the job of translation or, in technical terms, *conversion*; such a device is called *gateway*. The functionality of the protocol conversion or translation can be required at different levels or layers; hence, gateways can belong to different layers. For example, we can say that a modem works as a physical layer gateway device. The common practice while designing a computer network is to follow the same protocol in the entire network attached to a single router. Hence, the need of a gateway usually arises when two routers (following different protocols/standards) are connected together. In such a situation, the functionality of the gateway is implemented as an additional software component inside the router, resulting in a router working as a gateway too.

It is important to mention here that in most of the present-day computer networking scenarios, the devices that we see around us sometimes perform more than one of the above-mentioned roles. A very common example is the home routing device, which has the functionality of a bridge as well as a router. Similarly, the typical DSL modems available these days combine the functionality of a modem, bridge, gateway, as well as router.

1.2 Medium

The computer network medium is of two major types: wire and wireless. As the name suggests, in the wired medium the message propagates in a physical *wire* used to connect the devices. In a wireless medium, on the other hand, the message propagates in free space in the form of radio or infrared waves.

1.2.1 Wired Networks

Copper wire is the most common form of medium used in the wired computer networks. Coaxial and twisted pair cables are the two widely used copper wire or cable types. In dial-up Internet access, plain old telephone service lines are used to connect a computer to the Internet. The plain old telephone service lines are also copper wires and a computer requires a modem to communicate over this kind of wire. The fourth common type is the fiber optic cable, a thin cable or fiber of glass or plastic that works as a *pipe of light*.

> *Twisted pair.* As the name suggests, a twisted pair cable is made of thin copper wires twisted together. Multiple pairs of wires, shielded or unshielded, are bundled together in a cable. Twisted pair cable is the most widely used cable type for computer networks and telephone networks due to its lower cost and easy handling. It has several types and categories, based on quality, construction, purpose, and data rate supported. The highest-grade twisted pair cables can achieve data rates up to 1 Gbps;

however, most of the variations can carry signals up to 100 m without significant strength loss.

Coaxial. The coaxial cable has a copper wire in the center with a layer of insulation around it. Around this insulation layer, there is another layer of copper in the form of a gauze and a final outer insulation jacket. It was a common type of computer networking cable before the introduction of twisted pair cables. Still, it is commonly used for cable TV and cable Internet.

Fiber optic. In fiber optic cable, the signal is transmitted in the form of a light beam or wave inside the glass or plastic fiber. Multiple fibers are bundled together usually in a cable. A single fiber can carry multiple light waves, and it is possible to achieve very high data rates from each wave as compared to the copper wires. Furthermore, the effect of interference and attenuation is very low, which makes it possible to transmit the signal over longer distances. Due to its very high data rates and higher cost, fiber optic cable is not used to interconnect individual computers; rather it is used to combine networks.

1.2.2 Wireless Networks

Wireless networks are of two major categories: in the first, radio waves carry the data; in the second infrared waves carry the data. The radio-based wireless networks are more common since the infrared waves can only travel in a straight line and cannot penetrate through walls. One important characteristic of the wireless medium is that it is always shared because the signal travels in open space, which is accessible to all.

1.3 Network Topology

Network topology could be either physical or logical. A physical topology describes how the devices are physically linked with each other and what kind of medium is used for those links. The logical topology, on the other hand, is an abstract view of the physical topology with unnecessary details hidden. Thus, a physical topology can have multiple logical topologies produced after filtering the irrelevant details. The relationship between the two terms can be better described with the example of a layout or plan for a building. A detailed plan of a building will have all the details such as walls, doors, electric wiring, water lines, and sewer lines, just the way a physical topology has all the details of the computer network. However, we can also have a layout of electric wiring only for a building; such a plan is analogous to the logical topology in computer networks. Devices in a computer can be interconnected using different approaches; hence, it is possible to have different kinds of physical topologies.

The area physically covered by a computer network is another important aspect with respect to the topology. Primarily, it is due to the varying technical limitations of different media types. A classical approach to classify the networks is based on the geographical area covered by them. Local area network (LAN), metropolitan area network (MAN), and wide area network (WAN) are the three main categories. In the beginning, LANs, MANs, and WANs were distinguished based on the area covered; the administrative boundaries of a network and the relevance in the purpose of the devices participating in the network are some of the additional factors that contribute to decide the category to which a network belongs.

1.3.1 Wide Area Network

A WAN is a network that comprises devices distributed over a vast area, for example, a state or a continent, or even bigger. Thus, the Internet is usually referred to as a WAN; in fact, it is the largest WAN. Similarly, the nationwide network of some Internet service provider is also an example of WAN.

1.3.2 Local Area Network

A LAN is usually limited to a building or a group of adjacent buildings under one administration. The geographical limits of LAN are not that precise and terms such as *campus area network* are also used in situations when the area covered by a LAN is significantly large. However, technically, a network is considered a LAN when all the participating devices are interconnected using privately laid physical topology and is under one administration. This definition also leads us to the conclusion that when an organization's business is spread over a metropolitan area or wide area, in almost all the cases the organization's MAN or WAN is *logically* spread over the physical network laid by some other organization, usually the owner of the public telephone and data networks in that area.

The protocols and technologies used in LANs and WANs are also different, once again mainly due to the different attenuation features of the physical medium used.

1.4 Network Protocols and Standards

Although devices and medium are the physical components of a computer network, the importance of protocols is no less in the success of communication, as devices require a well-established plan to follow. Protocols describe actions to be performed and guidelines to be followed by the devices during communication. As mentioned earlier, the OSI reference model is the fundamental document of communication in computer networks. Protocols in most of the cases target the work plan of the OSI model; however, there is no single protocol that targets all the seven layers of the OSI model. A single protocol usually targets the job of an individual layer and protocols are always associated with the respective OSI layer. In order to perform communication, a device follows multiple protocols, which work in a cooperative fashion. This necessitates that protocols should be compliant to each other. Due to this fact, protocols evolve in the form of families or groups, where a family constitutes of protocols belonging to different OSI layers and compliant to each other.

The category of protocols and standards is in fact very rich and endless; however, in this section, we will limit our discussion to the relevant items from this list. The term *standard* in computer networks loosely refers to a protocol or model or an architecture or a combination thereof that is designed or ratified by some established authority or organization, such as IEEE, for wider commercial use.

ASSEMBLY OF A MESSAGE

An important principle to consider while reviewing the protocols is how a message is assembled before its actual transmission over the medium. In our communication model, it is in fact the user who wants to send a message using his or her device. This message is captured by some application on the device and will now go through a series of the protocols. Every protocol before passing on this message to the next protocol in the chain arranges the content of the message in a particular order usually referred to as *protocol data unit* (PDU) or sometimes simply a *packet*. Hence, PDU is a collection of bits or bytes or characters pertaining to the user message and some additional information for the convenience of the next protocol. This additional administrative information is usually placed in the beginning of the PDU and hence called the *header* of the PDU. In most of the cases, the next protocol in the chain only looks into the header for the necessary information and do not parse rest of the PDU.

1.4.1 IEEE 802 Standards Family

The IEEE 802 is a group of standards for LANs and MANs. It targets the communication tasks belonging to the first two layers of the OSI model. The IEEE 802 LAN and MAN reference model further divides the data link layer into two sub layers: medium access control (MAC) and logical link control, as shown in Figure 1.2 [1].

The IEEE 802 LANs and MANs are packet-based networks where message is transmitted as a sequence of data octets; most of the commercially available devices and applications are supported by these standards. The packets are technically referred to as *frames* at this level. The MAC sublayer is primarily responsible for the connectionless frame transfer between the two devices, while logical link control is more concerned with the services such as management, security, or acknowledgment (Figure 1.3) [1].

The IEEE 802 standards family has individual standards for several types of physical medium, as displayed in Figure 1.4. Each standard is

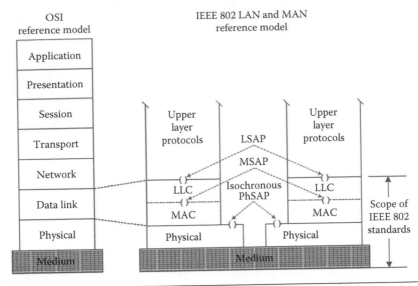

Figure 1.2 IEEE 802 LAN and MAN reference model for end stations. LLC—logical link control, MAC—medium access control, LSAP—link service access point, MSAP—MAC service access point, and PhSAP—physical service access point. (Data from *IEEE Standard for Local and Metropolitan Area Networks: Overview and Architecture*, IEEE Std 802®-2001 [R2007].)

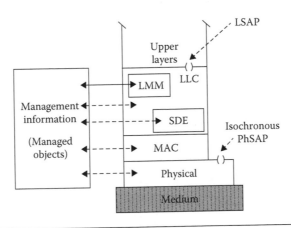

Figure 1.3 IEEE 802 reference model with end-station management and security. LMM—LAN/MAN management and SDE—secure data exchange. (Data from *IEEE Standard for Local and Metropolitan Area Networks: Overview and Architecture*, IEEE Std 802®-2001 [R2007].)

a collection of protocols and guidelines for a certain physical medium and the relevant MAC layer, for example, Ethernet, wireless LAN, and broadband wireless MANs. All kinds of MAC provide a common service with core features to the logical link control through the MAC service access point [1].

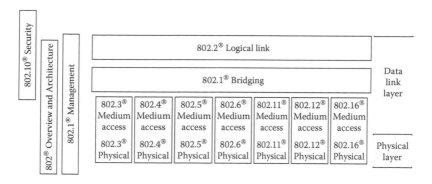

Figure 1.4 IEEE 802 standards family. (Data from *IEEE Standard for Local and Metropolitan Area Networks: Overview and Architecture*, IEEE Std 802®-2001 [R2007].)

Originally, the standard viewed LAN as a peer-to-peer communication network with shared medium and information broadcasted to all the stations. However, later the use of bridges for the interconnection of LANs and related features are also included. In fact, the ability to communicate directly without any intermediate switching node is the second distinguishing point in the IEEE definition of LAN and MAN, after the difference in their geographical area. Within its scope, the standard discusses two types of LAN interconnecting devices: bridges (discussed in Section 1.1) for MAC layer interconnectivity and repeaters and hubs for physical layer interconnectivity. In order to understand the difference between the two categories, we need to review the term *access domain* [1].

Access domain. A group of devices and media in a LAN or MAN where a single MAC protocol is being used and the medium is shared among all the devices is called *access domain*. In such a situation, at most one device transmits and all the other connected to the medium receive. A repeater connects the two LANs in such a way that both become one single access domain, implying when one device, from any participating LAN, transmits all the other devices on all the connected LANs will receive. Repeaters are useful when we are interested in increasing the range of a LAN, may be due to the technological limitations of the media such as signal attenuation. The term *hub* is used to refer to repeaters when the devices in a LAN are connected using star-wired topology [1].

MAC bridges. Following up from our earlier introduction of the bridges in Section 1.1, the IEEE 802 standard refers to the bridges as devices that interconnect two or more LANs at the MAC layer level but keep them as separate access domains. A bridge operates at the MAC layer and remains transparent to the logical link control and any other upper layers. Although, a device can communicate with any other device from any participating LAN, the message is heard usually only in the LAN to which the sender belongs and to which the receiver belongs and the rest of the LANs do not observe this transmission (Figure 1.5). Bridges relay or filter the messages heard on some LAN to the other LAN(s), if necessary. The relaying and filtering is based on the destination address and the source address stored in the frame header [1].

MAC addresses. According to IEEE 802 standard, every device* in a LAN or MAN is identified by a 48-bits address, usually referred to as the *MAC address.* Each device has a unique MAC address[†] so that the device can be properly distinguished.

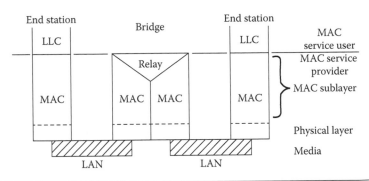

Figure 1.5 Internal organization of MAC sublayer with bridging. (Data from *IEEE Standard for Local and Metropolitan Area Networks: Overview and Architecture*, IEEE Std 802®-2001 [R2007].)

---

* The term *device* here technically means *interface of a device.* Since a device can have more than one network interfaces, each of these interfaces will have its own MAC address. However, it is possible that at the upper layers, all these separate data streams are combined for one single communication purpose. For example, routers usually have multiple interfaces and the job of forwarding is performed by relaying a packet—received on one of the interfaces—to a suitable interface.

† In fact, if a device has interfaces to more than one LAN then each interface has its own MAC address. This is why each port of a bridge has a different address and that port is considered part of the LAN to which it is attached.

MAC addresses are used in the frame headers to describe the source and the destination devices and used by bridges to filter and relay the frames [1].

Ethernet. Ethernet is one of the many physical (PHY)/MAC standards belonging to the IEEE 802 family. It is the most widely used technology for establishing wired LANs. Originally invented with the name *Ethernet*, IEEE formally ratified it as *IEEE Standard 802.3.* At the physical layer, Ethernet supports several twisted pair cable categories as well as the coaxial cable, and operational speeds from 1 Mbps to 100 Gbps. The MAC protocol is based on the carrier sense multiple access with collision detection (CSMA/CD) principle and has provision for both half duplex and full duplex transmission [2].

In Ethernet, devices send messages in the form of frames with the length commonly from 512 to 1518 octets. The frame contains several fields such as source address, destination address, actual data length, actual data, which is usually an upper layer packet, and frame check sequence. A detailed generic frame is described in Figure 1.6 [2].

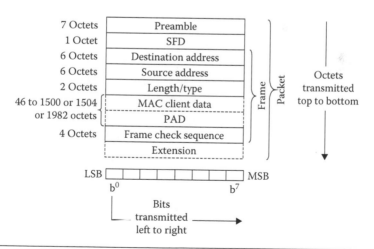

Figure 1.6   Ethernet packet format. (Data from *IEEE Standard for Ethernet*, IEEE Std 802.3-2012.)

 The Ethernet and 802.3 are generally considered the same standard these days. However, they have minor technical differences in their original design.

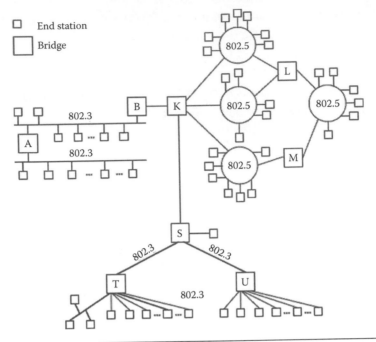

Figure 1.7   A bridged LAN. (Data from *IEEE Standard for Local and Metropolitan Area Networks: Overview and Architecture*, IEEE Std 802®-2001 [R2007].)

Bridging LANs. Figure 1.7 describes a typical IEEE 802 LAN where several smaller LANs are connected through bridges. As can be seen in the figure, bridges have multiple interfaces or ports through which they are connected to multiple LAN segments. Furthermore, a bridge can support more than one IEEE PHY/MAC standards if it is connecting two different types of IEEE PHY/MAC LANs* [3].

As mentioned earlier, bridges join the LAN segments into one but keep them as separate access domains through the actions of relaying and filtering. In addition to the relaying and filtering of frames, collecting and updating the necessary information for the purpose of relaying and filtering as well as management are also among the duties of bridges. One important aspect to consider here, in relation to Figure 1.7, is the following: when a bridge joins LAN segments that are

---

* Although not displayed in the figure, bridges, if required, also support IEEE wireless PHY/MAC standards.

following different LAN standards, it requires that the interface of the bridge to which a particular LAN is connected supports the standard being used in that LAN segment. Hence, an Ethernet segment can only be connected to the Ethernet port of the bridge and an 802.5 segment can only be connected through the 802.5 port of the bridge [3].

1.4.2 Internet Protocol Suite

The Internet protocol suite is a family of upper layer (network and above) protocols designed with the objective to provide end-to-end delivery of messages between two hosts, connected directly or indirectly through some other devices, in a network of any size. Commonly known as *transmission control protocol (TCP)/Internet protocol (IP) suite* due to the two major protocols of the family, TCP and IP, this protocol family is an outcome of the research initiative taken by DARPA and later joined by several other contributors.

The TCP/IP suite follows its own network model, which in fact is designed before the OSI reference model. In contrast to the OSI model, this model has four layers, as shown in Figure 1.8.

The network interface layer actually represents the two lower layers of the OSI model and is beyond the scope of the IP suite since this protocol family is designed to principally support all kinds of underlying physical network technologies. One important point to understand in the context of layering is that protocols and standards do not strictly follow the conceptual layer boundaries of the OSI model; the job description of a protocol often covers duties that are listed in more

OSI model	Internet layer
Application layer Presentation layer Session layer	Application layer
Transport layer	Transport layer
Network layer	Internet layer
Physical layer Data link layer	Network interface

Figure 1.8   OSI model versus the Internet model.

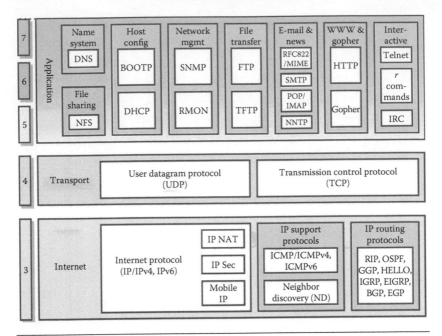

Figure 1.9 Internet protocol family.

than adjacent layers or more than one protocol support each other to perform the tasks recommended for a certain layer. Figure 1.9 displays several protocols belonging to this family and their position in the layered model.

In this review, once again, we will focus on the protocols and issues that are important and relevant to our main discussion.

Internet protocol. The IP [4] is the spirit of the Internet and the mighty that connects everyone on the Internet. The Internet model follows the principle that the IP will determine how a datagram will be transmitted when two hosts are communicating over an Internet, that is, a collection of smaller networks (probably LANs), that may or may not be under single administration, may or may not be using the same technologies, and may be very distant from each other. This includes activities such as determining the suitable routes and performing necessary administrative and management tasks. Since the route may consists of multiple hops, the datagram* is eventually delivered

---

* A packet or PDU of Internet Protocol is commonly called Datagram.

hop-by-hop with the help of the underlying network interface layer or the link layer. Hence, the IP provides a protocol and technology-independent end-to-end connectivity between the two end devices. This job is not as simple as it seems and involves the support of several other principles and protocols. Another important principle related to the job of the IP is the *best-effort delivery*, which means, while delivering a packet from the source to the destination, the IP keeps the things simple and does not provide any fancy service guarantees.

So how does the IP work? When the IP module of a source device receives a packet from the upper layer (a suitable layer/module as per Figure 1.8), the address of the destination device is usually specified in that packet. To its support, the IP has suitable routing protocols that determine for a given destination a suitable next hop device. This information of destinations and the suitable next hops for these destinations is placed in the routing tables that are consulted by the IP. Hence, by looking at the destination IP in the packet to be sent and consulting the routing table, the IP determines the next hop device; after performing the necessary steps of packet formation, it delivers the packet to the link layer for the delivery to this next hop device. The core procedure of the IP here is quite simple, that is, to forward the packet to the next hop device after consulting the routing table; but as we said earlier, the IP alone cannot do this job.

IP addressing. As we mentioned earlier, the Internet model is built on the notion of internet—a network of networks. Hence, the designers have incorporated to this model an addressing scheme that is independent of lower layer technologies and protocols, but provides a mean to group the devices in a hierarchical fashion, that is, the devices in the same network will be assigned addresses from the same range for easy identification and each network will use a different range of addresses for easy distinguishableness.

The IP has two versions: IPv4 and IPv6. One major enhancement done in IPv6 is the extension of address size

from 32 bits to 128 bits. Typically, for the readability purpose, a 32-bit-long IPv4 address is written as a string of four
decimal numbers separated by a *dot* (.), where each number
represents 8 bits in the address. On the other hand, 128-bit-
long IPv6 addresses are usually written as a string of 8 hexadecimal numbers separated by a *colon* (:), where each number
represents 16 bits in the address.*

Transmission control protocol. The IP family provides two different
options at the transport layer: TCP and user datagram protocol (UDP). TCP is designed with the objective to provide a
connection-based data transmission service between the two
end devices with certain service guarantees such as successful
delivery, flow control, and congestion control. Generally, the
choice of selecting TCP or UDP is made by the application
layer as per its service requirements. For example, the hypertext transfer protocol (HTTP) used in web browsing is based
on the TCP. TCP is further described in Section 1.5.2.

User datagram protocol. The UDP [10], on the other hand, provides a connection-less best-effort service with no guarantees at
all. Still there are application scenarios where the use of UDP
makes more sense; hence, UDP is still there in the market. For
example, the Dynamic Host Configuration Protocol (DHCP)
service that is used by a device to automatically acquire an IP
address on a certain network uses UDP protocol.

Routers. Before we finish our review of the basic networking concepts, it is important to have another look at the routers under
the light of the Internet model and the TCP/IP suite. Routers
are an important component of the Internet, a WAN based on
the Internet model, as they are the point through which each
LAN is connected to the complete WAN, that is, the end user
devices in some private network communicate with the rest of
the Internet through the routers. This leads us to the picture of
the Internet as a network of several interconnected networks,
of varying sizes, with each network tapping into the Internet
with its router, as described in Figure 1.10. Thus, the router is the

---

* Since one hexadecimal digit is equal to four binary digits, each number will have
four hexadecimal digits.

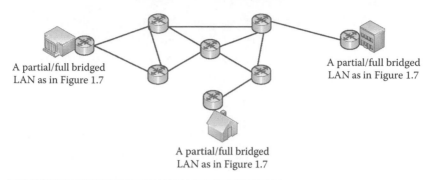

A partial/full bridged
LAN as in Figure 1.7

A partial/full bridged
LAN as in Figure 1.7

A partial/full bridged
LAN as in Figure 1.7

Figure 1.10   Physical model of the Internet.

entry/exit point of all the traffic between the local network and
the rest of the Internet. This fact places plenty of workload on
the routers, particularly the exit/entry routers, usually referred to
as *egress/ingress routers*, and makes their importance in the communication manifold. In the beginning, the basic tasks of the
routers were to identify the communication routes and to provide the interoperability for different protocols and technologies.
But with such a strategic location in the topology, routers these
days also play a significant role in traffic analysis and filtration.

Another important fact regarding the Internet architecture
described in Figure 1.10 is that in the core we have a mesh of
devices mainly to provide interconnectivity. This core is actually the service infrastructure provided by several Internet
service providers of different level and scale.

1.5 Common Network Protocols

In Chapters 2 and 3, we will focus on the information security and
the approaches that are used to breach the security of an information
system. The IP suite is a public group of protocols widely practiced in
the computer networks and very often the target of hacking attacks.
Before we conclude our review of the computer networks, it will be
very useful for the reader to have a brief technical review of some of
these important protocols.

1.5.1 Hypertext Transfer Protocol

The HTTP is an application layer protocol to share hyperme-
dia messages among systems. It is a generic protocol that does not

maintain state of the communication. It is the spirit of the World Wide Web service. The protocol has been improved over time to provide better features and support technological advancements; the three available versions are HTTP/0.9, HTTP/1.0, and HTTP/1.1, HTTP/1.1 being the latest [5].

The HTTP follows a request/response model where client initiates the communication by sending a request message to the server. The typical items included in this request message are request method, uniform resource identifier, protocol version, request modifiers, client information, and possible body content. The server responds to this request with a response message, which usually contains a status line, message's protocol version, a success or error code, server information, entity meta-information, and possible entity-body content [5].

HTTP communication is performed over TCP/IP connections with servers listening by default at TCP port 80. However, use of TCP is not compulsory and any transport protocol that provides reliable delivery can be used. In HTTP/1.0, by default, a new transport connection is used for each request/response exchange, while in HTTP/1.1, it is possible to use a connection for one or more request/response exchanges, usually referred to as *persistent behavior* [5].

HTTP has only two types of messages: request message sent by the client and response message sent by the server. The generic format of the two messages is displayed in Figures 1.11 and 1.12.

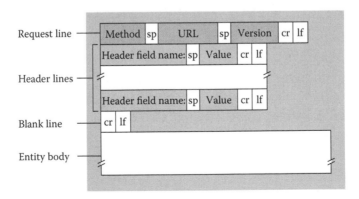

Figure 1.11   HTTP request message format.

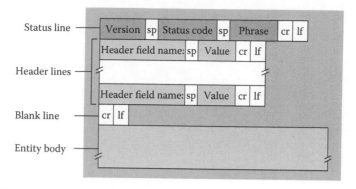

Figure 1.12 HTTP response message format.

1.5.2 Transmission Control Protocol

The TCP is an important core protocol from the IP suite designed to work at the transport layer and provide a reliable host-to-host service in packet-switched computer communication networks. It is a connection-oriented end-to-end protocol and supports multinetwork applications. The TCP provides reliable, ordered, and error-checked interprocess delivery of stream of octets between pairs of processes running in host computers attached to interconnected computer communication networks. Other features of the TCP include flow control and congestion control, but no security or bandwidth guarantees [6].

TCP is a combination of several algorithms and procedures that can be discussed; however, we will limit the review to the segment structure and the connection establishment in the following review.

> *TCP segment structure.* Unlike HTTP, where we have two separate message types, the purpose of a TCP segment is described through the selection of flags in the segment header. There are six basic flags that are defined in request for comments (RFC) 793 [6]*:
> - URG: Urgent pointer field significant
> - ACK: Acknowledgment field significant
> - PSH: Push function
> - RST: Reset the connection
> - SYN: Synchronize sequence numbers
> - FIN: No more data from sender

---

* In some later recommendations to improve the functionality of the TCP such as RFC 3168 and RFC 3540, some additional flags have been defined.

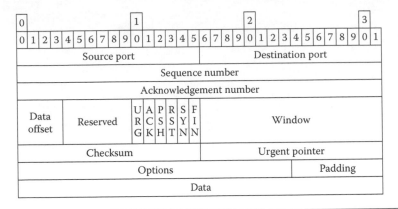

Figure 1.13 TCP segment format.

Most of the fields in this segment (Figure 1.13) are self-descriptive and generic in nature. However, the implementation of the sequence number field is host dependent and can be exploited by the intruders. Every TCP segment is assigned a sequence number by the host originating this segment, so that the different segments sent by this host can be properly ordered by the recipient host and the duplicates can be removed. The selection of initial sequence number, that is, the number sent in the first segment generated by a host is usually dependent on the operating system implementation of TCP at that host. This phenomenon helps the intruders to understand the type of OS by observing the initial sequence number.

TCP connection setup. TCP uses a three-way handshake process to establish a connection before starting to transmit the data segments (see Figure 3.4). The process is initiated by the client host by sending a segment with only the SYN bit set to indicate the intention to establish a connection. The server, if interested, replies with a segment where both SYN and ACK bits are set to acknowledge the receipt of the segment as well as the intention to establish the connection. Finally, the client will acknowledge the receipt by sending a segment with ACK bit set [6] (Figure 1.14).

1.5.3 Dynamic Host Configuration Protocol

The DHCP [7] is a significant protocol as it is commonly used in LANs to automatically assign IP addresses to the newly arriving hosts, thus

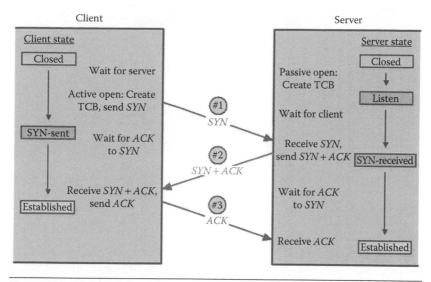

Figure 1.14   TCP three-way handshake connection setup.

avoiding the manual assignment by an administrator. DHCP is an application layer protocol that follows client-server model. However, unlike other client-server protocols, DHCP is connection less and uses UDP at the transport layer to deliver its messages. One or more DHCP servers are designated in the network by the administrator to dynamically allocate network addresses and deliver other configuration parameters when contacted by the dynamically arriving hosts.

Using DHCP an IP address can be allocated to a host in three possible ways. First, *automatic allocation* is possible to assign a permanent IP address to a host. Second, an IP address can be assigned to a client for a limited period of time, referred to as *dynamic allocation*. Finally, in *manual allocation*, the IP address assigned to the client is selected by the network administrator, and DHCP's job is to simply convey this assignment.

How DHCP assigns an IP address. In DHCP, a client follows a four-step process to automatically acquire the IP address (Figure 1.15).

1. Hosts are usually configured by the user to use a static IP address or acquire an automatic assignment through the DHCP, the latter being the most common option. The client initiates the process by sending a DHCP discover message.

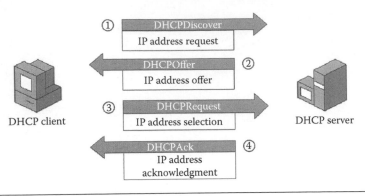

Figure 1.15   DHCP IP address allocation process.

Since the client is unaware of the IP address of the DHCP server(s), the IP address in this discover message is broadcast, that is, 255.255.255.255, the fact due to which this step is named as *discover*. DHCP servers are configured to listen at UDP port 67, while the client is required to select UDP port 68 as the source port. It might be possible that the DHCP server is not in the same subnet as the requesting host. In such a case, DHCP relay agents are placed in each subnet. The request to allocate an IP address is technically referred to as an *IP lease request*. Another important field in this request message is the client's MAC address.

2. Once the server receives the lease request, it sends a DHCP offer message to the client. The IP address offered in this request is selected following one of the three methods as per the server configuration for the client's MAC address. The important items in the DHCP offer message are the offered IP address, subnet mask, lease duration, and the server's own IP address. The destination IP address for this offer message is once again 255.255.255.255 the client so far has no IP address; the destination port is UDP 68 as mentioned earlier. In case there are more than one DHCP servers in the network, offers can be made by more than one servers. Another important issue to consider here is: if there are more than one clients waiting for the IP lease offer, how they identify that the offer is for whom when all

the offer messages are broadcast.* In order to distinguish among the different clients, a client randomly selects a transaction ID and specifies it in the DHCP discover message; all the follow up messages carry this transaction ID. DHCP relay agents will be involved again if the client and server are not in the same subnet.

3. Client will accept one of the offers and will generate a DHCP request message to acquire the IP address offered by the respective server. This message follows the same delivery configuration as the DHCP discover, that is, broadcasted due to the fact that all the DHCP servers should be duly informed that whose offer is accepted by the client and the others can withdraw their offers.

4. Finally, the DHCP server confirms the lease by sending a DHCP ACK message and other necessary configurations.

1.5.4 Internet Control Message Protocol

The Internet control message protocol (ICMP) [8] is used by the gateways or destination hosts to report an error in datagram processing to the source host. ICMP uses the datagram delivery service provided by the IP as if it were a protocol above it. ICMP is considered an integral part of the IP and is implemented by every IP module. The purpose of ICMP is not to make the IP reliable, rather to provide a mechanism to report the communication problems (Figure 1.16).

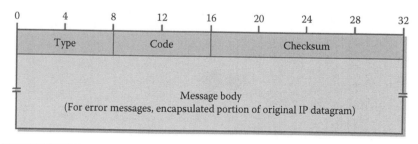

Figure 1.16 ICMP packet format.

---

* There are some cases when the DHCP offer is not broadcast, for example, when the client already has an IP address and is just requesting an extension in the lease.

ICMP messages are usually sent in the following situations:

- A datagram cannot reach the destination.
- The gateway does not have enough space in the buffer to forward a datagram.

For the purpose of feedback or error reporting, the type and the code fields combined have an extensive list of associated status codes; some important combinations are described in Table 1.1 [7].

Table 1.1   Important ICMP Type and Code Combinations

TYPE	CODE	DESCRIPTION
0—Echo reply	0	Echo reply (used to ping)
3—Destination unreachable	0	Destination network unreachable
	1	Destination host unreachable
	2	Destination protocol unreachable
	3	Destination port unreachable
	4	Fragmentation required, and DF flag set
	5	Source route failed
	6	Destination network unknown
	7	Destination host unknown
	8	Source host isolated
	9	Network administratively prohibited
	10	Host administratively prohibited
	11	Network unreachable for TOS
	12	Host unreachable for TOS
	13	Communication administratively prohibited
	14	Host precedence violation
	15	Precedence cutoff in effect
5—Redirect message	0	Redirect datagram for the network
	1	Redirect datagram for the host
	2	Redirect datagram for the TOS and network
	3	Redirect datagram for the TOS and host
8—Echo request	0	Echo request (used to ping)
11—Time exceeded	0	TTL expired in transit
	1	Fragment reassembly time exceeded
12—Parameter problem: bad IP header	0	Pointer indicates the error
	1	Missing a required option
	2	Bad length
13—Timestamp	0	Timestamp
14—Timestamp reply	0	Timestamp reply
17—Address mask request	0	Address mask request
18—Address mask reply	0	Address mask reply

1.5.5 Address Resolution Protocol

The address resolution protocol (ARP) [9] or more precisely the Ethernet ARP is another significant protocol in computer networks that develops the link between the IP addressing used by the family of internet protocols and the MAC addresses used in the network interface cards developed following the IEEE 802 standards. ARP is an independent protocol and is not part of any of the two groups; it is theoretically designed to work between any link layer standard and any network layer protocol.

Since ARP provides the link between the network layer and the data link layer, it itself works below the network layer and thus is not routable. This implies that the ARP packets are encapsulated directly inside the data link layer frames and can only travel within a LAN, but not beyond the router.

ARP has a single packet format in which different operations are specified by describing the suitable value in the operation field; for example, 1 is for the ARP request and 2 is for the ARP reply. The other two important fields are hardware type and protocol type. Hardware type specifies the hardware standard and ARP has a code list for different standards such as 0001 for Ethernet. Similarly, protocol type specifies the code of the network layer protocol, 0×0800 in case of IPv4 (Figure 1.17).

Address resolution process. The network layer datagram is handed over to the data link layer for transmission and the equivalent hardware address is required to mention in the frame

0	15	31
Hardware type (layer 2)		Protocol type (layer 3)	
Address length layer 2 (n)	Address length layer 3 (m)	Operation	
Source address (layer 2): n bytes			
Source address (layer 3): m bytes			
Destination address (layer 2): n bytes			
Destination address (layer 3): m bytes			

Figure 1.17 Generic ARP packet format.

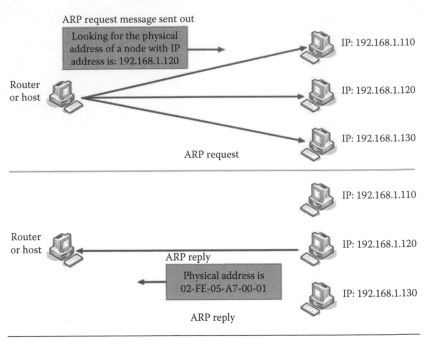

Figure 1.18   ARP address resolution process.

header for delivery. ARP maintains a cache or ARP table, where it stores the known network layer address to physical layer address mappings. In case the physical layer address for the network layer address is not present in the cache, an ARP request packet is broadcasted (MAC address with all ones) in the LAN including the network layer address for which the physical layer address is missing. Since it is a broadcast, every host on the LAN receives this frame and if the requested host is present, it will individually reply to the requesting host with its physical address through the reply message (Figure 1.18). The requesting host stores this entry in the ARP cache for future use. Additionally, the ARP request message helps the other hosts in the network to update the ARP entry for the source of the request.

References

1. *IEEE Standard for Local and Metropolitan Area Networks: Overview and Architecture*, IEEE Std 802®-2001 (R2007), https://standards.ieee.org/about/get/802/802.html.

2. *IEEE Standard for Ethernet*, IEEE Std 802.3-2012, https://standards. ieee.org/about/get/802/802.3.html.
3. *IEEE Standard for Local and Metropolitan Area Networks: Media Access Control (MAC) Bridges*, IEEE Std 802.1D-2004 (R2007), https://standards. ieee.org/about/get/802/802.1.html.
4. Postel, J., Internet Protocol, STD 5, RFC 791, DOI 10.17487/RFC0791, September 1981, http://www.rfc-editor.org/info/rfc791.
5. Fielding, R., Gettys, J., Mogul, J., Frystyk, H., Masinter, L., Leach, P., and T. Berners-Lee, Hypertext Transfer Protocol -- HTTP/1.1, RFC 2616, DOI 10.17487/RFC2616, June 1999, http://www.rfc-editor.org/ info/rfc2616.
6. Postel, J., Transmission Control Protocol, STD 7, RFC 793, DOI 10.17487/ RFC0793, September 1981, http://www.rfc-editor.org/info/rfc793.
7. Droms, R., Dynamic Host Configuration Protocol, RFC 2131, DOI 10.17487/RFC2131, March 1997, http://www.rfc-editor.org/info/ rfc2131.
8. Postel, J., Internet Control Message Protocol, STD 5, RFC 792, DOI 10.17487/RFC0792, September 1981, http://www.rfc-editor.org/info/ rfc792.
9. Plummer, D., Ethernet Address Resolution Protocol: Or Converting Network Protocol Addresses to 48.bit Ethernet Address for Transmission on Ethernet Hardware, STD 37, RFC 826, DOI 10.17487/RFC0826, November 1982, http://www.rfc-editor.org/info/rfc826.
10. Postel, J., User Datagram Protocol, STD 6, RFC 768, DOI 10.17487/ RFC0768, August 1980, http://www.rfc-editor.org/info/rfc768.

2

INFORMATION SYSTEM SECURITY

HABIB-UR REHMAN

Computer networks are a modern channel of communications: efficient, easy to use, and with plenty of options and variations. This communication, through these networks or any other approach, is always performed by the people and is meant for the people; we have many reasons to keep the communication secret. In this chapter, we will review the fundamentals of the communication security* in general and focus on the technical aspects in relation to the computer networks.

Before we begin, let us see how our communication model looks like

- Two or more devices are exchanging messages with each other.
- The messages could be either atomic or part of a longer communication.
- In case there are more than one recipient of the same message, this message can be transmitted individually to each of them or could be sent as a single broadcast.
- The participants of the communication can be in the same local network or may be in different local area networks that are connected through some suitable wide area network interface.

Since the message exchanged between two or more devices is certainly a piece of information, the principles established for information security are completely valid in our domain. Thus, the information security fundamentals are the perfect point to start this discussion.

---

* There are several aspects of security in the context of computers such as hardware and software; however, the focus of this book is on the communication performed using computers over the computer networks.

The researchers and professionals in the area of information security have suggested several models, which can be classified into two major categories. The first category is of general recommendations and guidelines to be followed to implement a secure information system. Three major examples from this group are as follows:

- Organisation for Economic Co-Operation and Development (OECD) Guidelines for the Security of Information Systems and Networks [1]
- National Institute of Standards and Technology (NIST) Engineering Principles for Information Technology Security [2]
- An Introduction to the Business Model for Information Security by Information Systems Audit and Control Association [3]

In the second category, there are models that describe the conceptual and technical elements of the information and provide recommendations based on these fundamental security characteristics of the information. Following are some popular models from the second category:

- CIA triad
- McCumber's Cube [4]
- Parkerian Hexad [5]
- Model for Information Assurance by Maconachy et al. [6]
- Reference Model of Information Assurance and Security [7]

In this chapter, we have reviewed the second category and have only discussed the security elements and characteristics of the information. Our objective here is to provide a quick review of the fundamental security concepts required to appreciate the importance and utility of intrusion detection and prevention in computer network communications.

2.1 CIA Triad

The CIA triad is the most fundamental model in information security that defines the core principles. The term *CIA** refers to the three basic characteristics or criteria of the security: confidentiality, integrity, and availability. The trio is a de facto standard for security, being in practice for such a long time that it is difficult to trace its origin.

---

* The most familiar use of the term CIA is for Central Intelligence Agency; hence, in the literature some authors have also used the term *AIC triad* to avoid the confusion.

Some even suggest that the existence of ciphers in the times of Julius Caesar indicates that the concept of confidentiality was well known even then. In the modern times, Saltzer and Schroeder appear to be the first ones describing* the three categories of security violations: unauthorized information release, unauthorized information modification, and unauthorized denial of use [8].

The three attributes (CIA) are considered the essential elements for the security of any kind of information system, including our communication over the computer networks. There are certainly several additions suggested to this list, but confidentiality, integrity, and availability are at the core of every extended model.

2.1.1 Confidentiality

In non-technical sense, confidentiality is equivalent to the term *privacy* that we use in daily life, that is, "no one should be able to know what I am up to provided, that is my personal matter." Technically, confidentiality is defined as the characteristic that only authorized people have access to the resource. Thus, it is the attribute of concealing the resources from unauthorized entities. In terms of information security, it is the assurance that the information would be available only to authorized people. This interpretation can be extended in several ways, which are as follows:

- The information will be stored in authorized form only, whether physical or electronic, and only authorized people will have access to the data stores.
- The information will be stored in authorized format only.
- The information will be available through authorized mediums only.

In case of our communication using computer networks, there are two major aspects of confidentiality. First, the confidentiality of the existence of communication, that is, only those who are authorized should be aware that communication is going on or has happened. Second, the confidentiality of the content of the communication, that is, only those who are authorized should be able to see what was communicated or is being communicated.

---

* In [9], Saltzer and Schroeder in fact have given the credit of this categorization to the other security specialists of that time, without clearly stating the exact source.

2.1.2 Integrity

The unauthorized access to a resource may lead to the problem of misusing it or corrupting it. In information security, integrity is the characteristic that information is not altered in an unauthorized manner. Thus, on one hand, it is the assurance that the information is in its original state without any corruption. On the other hand, it is also the affirmation that any modification required either has been made or will be made using an authorized approach such as only by authorized people and only using authorized means.

It is not necessary that unauthorized alteration to the information is always with malicious intent; it could be unintentional or accidental. For example, the communication over computer networks could have errors due to electronic malfunction. Integrity is the attribute that requires that the accuracy and consistency of the information should remain intact in all sorts of scenarios, whether malicious or accidental, intentional, or unintentional.

Although, it looks that unauthorized alteration always comes up with unauthorized access in its bag. However, there could be situations when the integrity of the information can be compromised without harming the confidentiality. A very simple example of this case is the bit error happened in a message sent over a computer network. Here the content of the message is not accessed by any unauthorized entity; however, its content is still altered.

2.1.3 Availability

The resource should be available to the authorized users when required. Availability is the attribute that the system provides the information to the authorized users or viewers whenever they are in need of it, usually all the time. Availability of information indirectly requires that

- The system storing the data/information should be available.
- The system used to retrieve the data/information should be available.
- The system used to update the data/information should be available.
- A backup plan should be available, and in case of failure, the backup system should be able to take control immediately.

The interruption in the availability can also be due to malicious intent or accidental causes. For example, a computer where the data is being stored can be physically damaged by an intruder or it could be out of order due to some electronic fault in the hardware. Availability is the guarantee that no matter what the reason is, authorized users will be able to access the information through usual means.

When communicating through computer networks, the nonavailability of the network resources or their inadequacy could also lead to the compromise of availability. For example, insufficient bandwidth can affect the service quality or some network services might not be available at all in some regions.

2.1.4 CIA Triad versus McCumber's Cube

McCumber's information security model or Cube has indeed the same three characteristics: confidentiality, integrity, and availability. However, his complete model has three dimensions where the above three characteristics represent only one dimension named as security characteristics or goals. The other two dimensions are information states and security safeguards or measures. The information is in three states as per the model: storage, processing, and transmission. The security measures are also of three main types: policy, education, and technology (Figure 2.1).

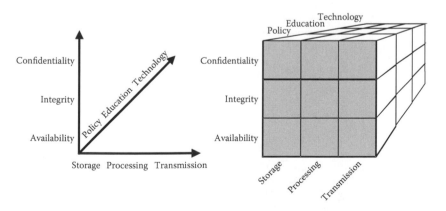

Figure 2.1 McCumber's Cube of information security. (Data from McCumber, J., Information systems security: A comprehensive model, in: *Proceedings of the 14th National Computer Security Conference*, NIST, Baltimore, MD, 1991.)

2.2 Parkerian Hexad

Donn B. Parker suggested a model with six fundamental security elements, usually referred to as *Parkerian Hexad*. In addition to the three attributes from the classical list of CIA, utility, authenticity, and possession are the new recommendations from Parker. He primarily feels that the three CIA attributes are not comprehensive and precise in terms of their definition and in-practice interpretations and thus, are inadequate to accommodate all the possibilities. Each of the three new attributes, hence, incorporate the security concerns not considered under the traditional interpretations of one of the CIA attributes [5,10] (Figure 2.2).

2.2.1 Possession

Parker elaborates that the possession of the information or having control over it is different than the confidentiality of the information because the unauthorized possession of the information can still be a security concern even if the person having control over it does not look into it. The confidentiality of the information in such a case itself is not harmed, but the violation of possession may lead to a confidentiality

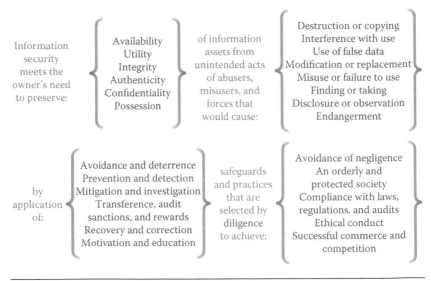

Figure 2.2 Parker's new fundamental conceptual information security model. (Data from D. Parker, Our excessively simplistic information security model and how to fix it, *ISSA J.*, 8 (7): 12–21, July, 2010.)

problem later. Hence, Parker believes that the inclusion of possession as a security attribute is necessary to avoid situations where the control over information can come into the hands of unauthorized entities intentionally, accidentally, or maliciously. The communication over computer networks is in fact a perfect example here because in most of the cases the physical network is publically accessible, implying that anyone can have the control over the on-going communication if proper measures are not adopted.

2.2.2 *Authenticity*

Authenticity of the information is defined as the validity of the source of the information or confirmation about the origin of the information. Thus, this characteristic describes whether the source of the information is the same as the recipient is expecting or assuming. Parker explains that authenticity is different from integrity, as the latter is about the soundness and condition of the information content. At times, an authorized source can generate incorrect information or the information that violates integrity for testing purposes, thus not violating the authenticity. On the other hand, a malicious source can pretend to be someone else, and thus reproduce a correct piece of information such as software with its own name but actually developed by a different entity. Parker further advocates that the measures required to mitigate the two issues are also different.

2.2.3 *Utility*

The final enhancement suggested by Parker is the utility, which he defines as the usefulness of data or information. Parker believes that the term *availability* is limited to the usability of the information, which not always guarantees that the information will be useful as well. For example, if the information is delivered in the encrypted form but the recipient has lost the decryption key, the information is still available but its utility is zero [10]. On the other hand, the above scenario complies with both availability and utility if the objective is to perform cryptanalysis. Thus, availability is only concerned about the access to the information, while utility is concerned about the convenience in its use and its comprehension.

2.2.4 CIA Triad versus Parkerian Hexad

The difference between the CIA triad and the Parkerian Hexad is primarily a difference of interpretations of the terms used. There is no doubt that the concerns mentioned by Parker are of less importance or do not exist; however, professionals over time have merged these extended interpretations into the three CIA attributes.

2.3 Model for Information Assurance

The model presented by Maconachy et al. [6] is indeed an extension of the McCumber's Cube. First, they have suggested a fourth dimension *time* to the model that indicates the security state of the system at different times. Second, they proposed two additional services in the security services dimension: authentication and non-repudiation.

It is difficult to identify the origin of the two terms *authentication* and *non-repudiation* as they have appeared in multiple sources around the same time. For example, we have seen the *authenticity* in Parker's Hexad. Maconachy et al. themselves in [6] have associated the two terms with a glossary of security terms [11] published by National Security Agency. Similarly, NIST has also described similar models in [12] (Figure 2.3).

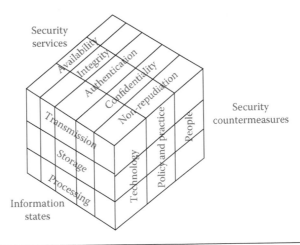

Figure 2.3 Information assurance model. (Data from Maconachy, W. et al., A model for information assurance: An integrated approach, in: *Proceedings of the IEEE Workshop on Information Assurance and Security*, U.S. Military Academy, New York, 2001.)

2.3.1 Authentication

The authentication in this model refers to a service to validate the *authenticity* in the Parker's model. Hence, it is the process or measure used to verify the validity of the originator of the information. The term in this model refers to the measure only and does not include the characteristics; however, the definition provided by NIST in [12] is not just limited to the validity of the source of the information; they have rather described it as a process to validate the identity of an entity. For example, the act of validating the authorization of a person to access a resource is also considered authentication.

2.3.2 Non-Repudiation

The one important issue that was missing in the CIA triad as well as in the Parker's Hexad is, What if one of the two parties sharing the information later denies the incident? Non-repudiation is a security objective introduced to overcome this concern and a system cannot be completely secure if there is no assurance that there will be necessary record keeping of a transaction, so that later none of the participants can deny its participation. In information sharing scenarios, for the sender, the assurance of a successful delivery to the correct recipient is necessary; for the receiver, the identity of the source is essential and in case there is a controlling authority involved, both the assurances are important. From the recipient's point of view, non-repudiation does not ensure that sender is the rightful owner of the information; that aspect is covered under authentication.

2.3.3 Non-Repudiation versus Accountability

In [11, p. 2], *accountability* is considered as one of the security goals by NIST and is defined as the "the requirement that actions of an entity may be traced uniquely to that entity." Non-repudiation, on the other hand, is described as a preventive service to achieve the goal of accountability [11]. Once again, it is a matter of different interpretations; the objective is to ensure that there is necessary evidence for future auditing.

2.4 Reference Model of Information Assurance and Security

Finally, Cherdantseva and Hilton in [7] proposed a very detailed model based on an extensive survey of existing work and models. The security goals described in this model have all the items we have described earlier, except privacy and auditability. The second difference is in the definitions used for accountability and non-repudiation. In their view, accountability is the characteristic of a system to hold users responsible for their actions, thus making it only applicable to humans. Non-repudiation to them is mainly record keeping of the occurring events with the details of parties involved (Figure 2.4).

2.4.1 Auditability

Auditability is defined as "an ability of a system to conduct persistent, non-bypassable monitoring of all actions performed by humans or machines within the system" [7, p. 7]. Thus, the actions performed by different entities will be observed and analyzed for their compliance with the rules and policies. The term *auditing* usually refers to a subsequent analysis of an event and it is not clear in [7] whether the term *auditability* carries the same sense or it refers to the live monitoring of events or both the cases.

2.4.2 Privacy

Privacy is the attribute that the owner of the information is able to control it and the spreading of the information complies with the privacy laws and owner's discretion. Privacy is sometimes confused with the confidentiality and integrity, as they all have the sense of obfuscating from *others*. Confidentiality is even required in circumstances when some public information is shared within a group or integrity is required for public content as well. On the other hand, a resource or information that is private is rarely shared and indeed this is the attribute that makes it private.

2.5 Fundamentals of Hacking

The fundamental concepts that are presented so far in this chapter are usually referred to as the necessary attributes that a secure information system should have or sometimes considered as the targets to achieve in order to make an information system secure. This is equally applicable to any computing system that generates, handles, stores, or

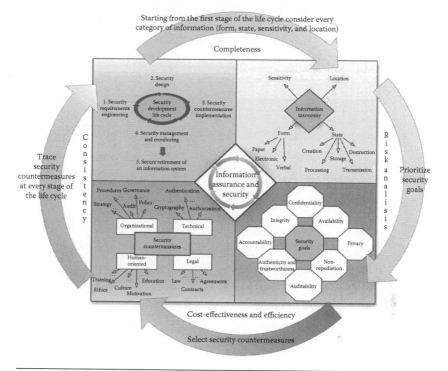

Figure 2.4 Reference model of information assurance and security. (From Y. Cherdantseva, and J. Hilton, A reference model of information assurance & security, in: *Proceedings of the Eighth International Conference on Availability, Reliability and Security (ARES)*, Regensburg, Germany, September 2–6, 2013.)

deals with information in any possible way. The intruder or a malicious entity is interested to affect the system and information handled by the system by compromising one or more of these security characteristics. Before we conclude this chapter, it would be very useful to review how the system can be attacked and revisit the elementary concepts of the dark science of hacking.

2.5.1 *Threats*

There are mainly three types of threats to an information system, which are as follows:

- *Natural threats*: These include natural disasters such as earthquakes, floods, or any other uncontrollable hazard.
- *Physical threats*: Damages can be happen due to fire, power, or water; this could be intentional or unintentional.

- *Human threats*: The insiders or outsiders can harm the system, intentionally or unintentionally, with the malicious intent or under the influence of disgruntlement. Humans can threaten the system in three possible ways, which are as follows:
    - *Network threats*: As we mentioned earlier, computer networks are the most common medium to share information. An intruder can break into the communication channel to compromise the security in several ways.
    - *Host threats*: The hosts dealing with the information can be directly attacked and their security can be breached.
    - *Application threats*: Applications processing the information if not properly developed might have vulnerabilities that can be exploited by the intruders.

In Chapter 3, we have presented a comprehensive list of several attacks, belonging to the above three categories, with their technical details.

2.5.2 Hacking Process

Intruders exploit the vulnerabilities of a system to launch an attack on the system. These vulnerabilities can be in the individual application or in the host as a whole or could be in the network through which the hosts will share the information. The process of launching an attack is usually divided into the following steps:

- *Reconnaissance*: The initial phase where intruder collects necessary information about the system and develops the attack strategy based on this initial data. Reconnaissance could be active where intruder interacts with the system or could be passive where the data is collected through indirect sources such as social engineering or dumpster diving or going through public resources. Footprinting is a common reconnaissance technique with both active and passive methods to gather the data on the system.
- *Scanning*: Active reconnaissance and scanning are not very different concepts as both collect the information about the system and its resources through interaction. Although the

intruder interacts with the system, scanning is not considered the actual attack on the system as the intruder does not harm the system or information. It is rather the process of identifying the network and host vulnerabilities.

- *Gaining access*: This phase refers to the step where the intruder attempts to access the network, or the host or the application by exploiting the discovered vulnerabilities.
- *Maintaining access*: Once the intruder has successfully accessed the resource, it is the time to use the resources of the system to collect the required information or to launch further attacks.
- *Clearing tracks*: The last act is to hide the malicious actions from the authorized users and the administrators. Usually, this is performed by destroying the evidence in the log files and archives.

After looking at the above phases, the term *attack* becomes fuzzy. In the literature, there are two interpretations in practice. It may refer to an individual malicious action of small scale or could be a large hacking activity performed through a series of small-scale intrusions. Thus, we can say that scanning itself is an attack as well as a phase of a hacking attack.

> *Scanning versus enumeration.* Scanning and enumeration are the two techniques that belong to the second phase of hacking, that is, scanning; confused? Surprisingly, the hacking industry has picked the same word for a hacking phase and a technique used in that phase, mainly due to the reason that again enumeration is very similar to scanning. However, the objective in enumeration is to discover user names, machine names, shared resources, services, and other similar entities. Scanning, on the other hand, is performed to discover active network hosts and open ports on these hosts, thus, referred to as *network scanning* too.

References

1. Organisation for Economic Co-Operation and Development (OECD). *OECD Guidelines for the Security of Information Systems and Networks: Towards a Culture of Security*, Organisation for Economic Co-Operation and Development, Paris, France, July 25, 2002. http://www.oecd.org/sti/ieconomy/15582260.pdf.

2. G. Stoneburner, C. Hayden, and A. Feringa *Engineering Principles for Information Technology Security (A Baseline for Achieving Security), Revision A*, Computer Security Division, Information Technology Laboratory, National Institute of Standards and Technology, Gaithersburg, MD, June 2004.
3. ISACA, *An Introduction to the Business Model for Information Security*, ISACA, Rolling Meadows, IL, 2009.
4. J. McCumber, Information systems security: A comprehensive model, in: *Proceedings of the 14th National Computer Security Conference*, NIST, Baltimore, MD, 1991.
5. D. Parker, *Fighting Computer Crime*, John Wiley & Sons, New York, 1998.
6. W. Maconachy, C. Schou, D. Ragsdale, and D. Welch, A model for information assurance: An integrated approach, in: *Proceedings of the IEEE Workshop on Information Assurance and Security*, U.S. Military Academy, New York, 2001.
7. Y. Cherdantseva, and J. Hilton, A reference model of information assurance & security, in: *Proceedings of the Eighth International Conference on Availability, Reliability and Security (ARES)*, Regensburg, Germany, September 2–6, 2013.
8. J. Saltzer, and M. Schroeder, The protection of information in computer systems, *Proceedings of the IEEE* 63(9), 1278–1308, 1975.
9. Y. Cherdantseva, and J. Hilton, *Reference Model of Information Assurance & Security*, http://rmias.cardiff.ac.uk/, March 29, 2015.
10. D. Parker, Our excessively simplistic information security model and how to fix it, *ISSA Journal* 8(7), 12–21, July, 2010.
11. National Security Agency, *National Information Systems Security Glossary*. NSTISSI 4009, National Security Agency, Fort Meade, MD, September 2000.
12. G. Stoneburner, NIST Special Publication 800-33: *Underlying Technical Models for Information Technology Security*, Recommendations of the National Institute of Standards and Technology, Gaithersburg, MD, December 2001.

3

INTRUSIONS AND VULNERABILITIES

HABIB-UR REHMAN

Securing the communication and its content is an important concern in computer networks due to the fact that most of the physical infrastructure is publicly accessible and shared among the users. This fact brings all the security goals into play, which we have described in Chapter 2. Furthermore, we have reviewed in Chapter 1 that most of the protocols used to deliver messages between the end hosts are public. Thus, everyone is aware of the sequence of actions that will be performed while transmitting a message and could exploit this knowledge to attack the ongoing communication. This simply does not mean that nothing is secure in computer networks; protocols have evolved to overcome such deficiencies. However, the service model of the computer networks in general and the Internet in particular, is developed or evolved in such a way that it is impossible to eliminate all the weaknesses.

An intruder exploits the vulnerabilities of a system to launch an attack against it; this makes it extremely important for the administrators and the rightful users of the system to be well aware of these vulnerabilities. The network, the hosts, and the applications running on the hosts can be misused if not properly designed and configured. The purpose of this chapter is to highlight such issues at all the three levels. We have attempted to compile a comprehensive list of commonly known attacks possible.

3.1 Network and Protocol Vulnerabilities

Public protocols and their vulnerabilities are indeed the biggest source of attacks in computer networks. This section discusses the commonly known attacks possible on the protocols such as hypertext markup

45

language (HTTP) [1], simple mail transfer protocol (SMTP) [5], transmission control protocol (TCP) [2], user datagram protocol (UDP) [3], Internet control message protocol (ICMP) [4], and others. This list indeed indicates the vulnerabilities in these commonly used protocols that can be exploited to launch different types of attacks.

3.1.1 HTTP Banner Grabbing

World Wide Web is a public service; therefore, the hosts running web servers are configured to allow any incoming requests to the port 80, the well-known port for the Web service. HTTP, the protocol used for the Web service is designed to reply to every HTTP request message with an HTTP response message. Usually, this response message contains the main/default page (mostly named as index*) of the requested website. In Figure 3.1, the HTTP response header fields for a certain website are displayed.

```
[HTTP/1.1 200 OK]
X-SharePointHealthScore : [0]
MicrosoftSharePointTeamServices : [15.0.0.4569]
Content-Length : [77244]
Expires : [Mon, 16 Mar 2015 20:56:19 GMT]
Last-Modified : [Tue, 31 Mar 2015 20:56:19 GMT]
request-id : [bb3cf89c-0754-5066-7cad-fac0a26769a5]
Connection : [keep-alive]
Server : [Microsoft-IIS/8.0]
X-Powered-By : [ASP.NET]
X-Content-Type-Options : [nosniff]
Cache-Control : [private, max-age=0]
SPRequestGuid : [bb3cf89c-0754-5066-7cad-fac0a26769a5]
SPIisLatency : [0]
X-AspNet-Version : [4.0.30319]
Date : [Tue, 31 Mar 2015 20:56:18 GMT]
Vary : [Accept-Encoding]
X-FRAME-OPTIONS : [SAMEORIGIN]
X-MS-InvokeApp : [1; RequireReadOnly]
Content-Type : [text/html; charset=utf-8]
SPRequestDuration : [399]
```

Figure 3.1 Typical HTTP response message.

Banner grabbing is classified as a preattack[*] or reconnaissance technique in hacking, where a system on the network is accessed through its public services such as the Web to collect some important information about the system. An HTTP response, as in Figure 3.1, contains several important items in the HTTP message header or in the page contained in the message body that can be of interest to some attacker. For example, the *Server* field indicates the type of web server being used.

Such a banner grabbing attack is applicable to the email messages as well, where the header of the received email also contains fields with important information. However, the email scenario is different from the HTTP scenario as such an analysis can only be performed if one has an email in hand.

> *SMTP enumeration.* However, in the SMTP, the protocol used to deliver emails to mail servers, an intruder can use the commands VRFY, EXPN, and RCPT TO through interfaces such as Telnet prompt to identify which email addresses are valid and which are not valid. Thus, the intruder can develop a list of valid email addresses that can later be used for malicious activities such as Spam messaging.

3.1.2 HTTP Tunneling

Tunneling is an important concept in computer networks where the packet of one protocol is encapsulated inside the packet of another protocol. This approach is usually adopted when the protocol of the hidden/inside packet is not supported by the underlying network; usually, this could be due to some administrative restrictions, incompatible protocols, or device limitations. Tunneling increases the utility of the network as it makes the communication possible even if there are incompatibilities. For example, IPv6 datagrams can be shared between the end hosts connected through devices (some or all) not supporting IPv6 by establishing an IPv4 tunnel, from end to end or for fewer hops

---

[*] In hacking, reconnaissance techniques are further classified into groups such as footprinting, enumeration, or scanning. The banner grabbing attack, as described in the text, cannot be precisely placed into any of these subclasses as it achieves multiple purposes.

as per requirement. Tunneling can be performed at any layer or protocol. However, HTTP tunneling is a major concern as the HTTP messages are rarely filtered or blocked* to provide access to the Web. The most common use of HTTP tunneling is to avoid firewall restrictions for content, services, or protocols such as restricted websites and audio/video streaming restrictions. Secure Shell is another common application layer protocol that is used for tunneling purposes. However, in contrast to HTTP network, administrators quite often restrict the Secure Shell ports to avoid tunneling through Secure Shell.

HTTP tunneling is performed by using software designed to communicate through the HTTP. The client component of the software is installed on the user† machine, and it establishes an HTTP tunnel with the server component of the software installed on the servers of tunneling service provider, to which the access is not restricted. These servers relay the user request to the servers or services that are directly restricted. The response is relayed back to the user through the tunnel in the same fashion (Figure 3.2).

3.1.3 TCP Scanning

TCP is the most widely used transport layer protocol on the Internet as it provides reliable and in-order delivery, required by most of the applications. However, this costs in terms of operational complexity and a huge list of vulnerabilities. A TCP connection is established through a three-way handshake process before sending the actual application messages. Based on the behavior of the TCP, particularly during the connection

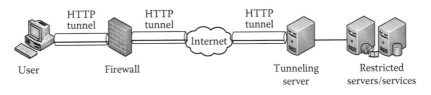

Figure 3.2   HTTP tunneling process.

---

* It is not that HTTP messages are never restricted. However, the usual scenario of restriction for HTTP traffic is to restrict HTTP requests for some known uniform resource locators (URL), which is not the case here.
† We have intentionally avoided the use of the word *attacker* here as not all the uses of HTTP tunneling are unanimously considered malicious.

establishment phase, there are several techniques that can be applied to reveal the details of the target network/hosts. One common approach is to send different types of TCP segments to the target host to identify the open/close status of the ports on the target. This attacking approach is usually referred to as *port scanning*.

> *TCP connect/full open scan.* The client host attempts to establish a proper TCP connection with the target host on a certain port. If the port is open for TCP services, the connection will be successfully established by performing the three-way handshake; otherwise, a TCP segment with the reset (RST) bit will be received indicating that the port is not open for connections (Figure 3.3b). This scan technique is also referred to as *Vanilla scan*, that is, when the intruder scans all 65,536 ports for Full Open scan. The regular TCP behavior, also followed in Full Open scan, is to respond with an acknowledgement (ACK) segment in step 3 and proceed with transmitting application messages (Figure 3.3a).
>
> *Slow scan.* Vanilla scan, that is, a scan of all the ports of a target system based on Full Open scan approach has a drawback that most of the hosts log the successful TCP connections; thus, an administrator can identify such an attack by observing the logs when he or she finds so many successful connection attempts on different ports. In order to avoid this problem, one approach is to attempt the next port after a reasonable

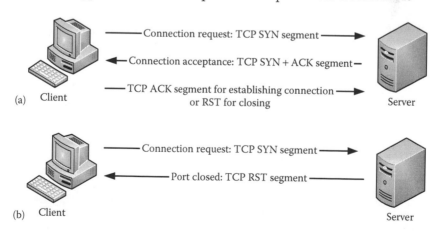

Figure 3.3 (a) TCP connection handshake when target port is open. (b) TCP connection handshake when target port is closed.

interval, that is, perform the scan at a slow pace. Slow scan is the simplest stealth scan approach.

Half open/syn scan. Another important aspect of the Full Open scan that can be easily followed in Figure 3.3 is that the third step of the handshake does not reveal any additional information on the port status. Hence, in synchronize (SYN scan, if the port is open, the client responds with a TCP RST segment to immediately destroy the ongoing connection request (Figure 3.3a). The SYN scan is also considered as one of the stealth scan approaches as it tries to avoid being noticed by the administrators.

Xmas or Xmas-tree scan. Xmas scan is another stealthy approach in which the client sends an invalid combination of TCP flags to the target host. If the target system is compliant with the TCP specifications as in RFC 793, it responds with a TCP RST segment in case of a closed port, or ignores the segment if the port is open. This attack usually works with UNIX hosts only; Windows machines always ignore such segments. There are two variations of the Xmas scan. The first variation uses only finish (FIN), urgent (URG), and push (PSH) flags, that is, sets these three flags in the segment. In the second variation, all the TCP flags are set (Figure 3.4).

FIN scan. FIN scan is an approach similar to the Xmas scan as it also uses an unexpected combination of TCP flags in the received segment. However, in FIN scan, only the FIN flag is set. Such a segment is unexpected because a FIN segment is usually sent to indicate the intention to close an established connection, while here there is no working connection between the client and the target. A closed port in such a case again responds with a TCP RST segment, while an open port ignores such segments.

Null scan. Null scan can be considered an approach opposite to the Xmas scan as in this case, the TCP segment sent has all

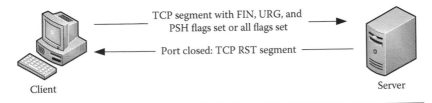

TCP segment with FIN, URG, and PSH flags set or all flags set

Port closed: TCP RST segment

Client

Server

Figure 3.4　TCP Xmas-tree scan process.

flags unset. Such a segment in the TCP is indeed a normal data segment transmitted after the successful connection establishment. Since the target host has no established connection with the client, it will discard the packet if the target port is open. In case, the port is closed, it will respond with a TCP RST segment. The success of the null scan depends on the implementation of the TCP stack in the target host and usually such segments are blocked on Microsoft platform.

Inverse flag scans. Xmas-tree, FIN, and null scans are also called *inverse or inverse flag scans* as in the case of these scans, a closed port at the target replies with a segment while an open port does not respond.

ACK scan. Another approach to exploit the target by sending an unexpected TCP segment is to set the ACK flag in the segment. An ACK segment is usually sent as the third step in the handshake process or to confirm the successful receipt of a data segment.* Since the target host does not identify any of the two cases, it will respond with the RST segment in case the port is not filtered no matter what the status of the port is. Thus, ACK scan is primarily useful to identify the behavior of firewall for certain ports. The analysis of the Window and time to live (TTL) fields can further help to identify the state of the port. Closed ports usually specify the Window size equal to 0, while open ports specify a nonzero Window size. Furthermore, the TTL value for the open ports is usually lower as compared to the TTL value for the open ports.

Fragmented scan. In order to avoid being detected by the firewalls, one approach that is used in different TCP scans to increase the effectiveness is to divide the TCP header into multiple Internet protocol (IP) fragments, that is, send the probe segment in multiple IP datagrams. Most of the intrusion detection systems are unable to detect a scan when the TCP header is fragmented.

Idle or dumb scan. Idle scan is a complex but smart attack, which is performed with the help of a third host usually referred to as

---

* An ACK flag is usually set in all the segments after the first two steps of the handshake process due to the fact that they are all acknowledgments.

a *dumb* or *zombie host*, due to its unintentional participation in the attack. The attack exploits the fact that all the IP datagrams generated by a host are assigned a *fragment identification number* and every new datagram has a fragment ID one more than the previously generated datagram. Hence, if host X is receiving from host Y IP datagrams with no gaps, this indicates that host Y is not communicating with any other host at the moment.

The intruder in case of an idle attack communicates with the dumb host and observes the increment in the IP fragment IDs; any inverse flag scan approach can be used for this purpose. The important point to consider while selecting a host as a zombie is that it is an idle host not generating any other IP traffic at the moment. Thus, when probed repeatedly, the IP datagrams sent by the zombie host will have continuous fragment IDs. The interesting fact regarding this attack is that the zombie host is not the actual target of the intruder. The intruder sends SYN segment to the actual target host but with the IP address of the zombie host, that is, spoofs the IP address. If the port is open at the target host, a SYN + ACK segment will be sent to the zombie host to which the zombie will reply with an RST segment, as it was never interested in the connection. This segment sent by the zombie to the target host will produce a gap in the IP fragment IDs that the intruder is observing through its probing of the zombie, indicating that the requested port at the target host is open (Figure 3.5).

TCP session hijacking. Session hijacking is an attack where an intruder maliciously takes over an ongoing communication session between two parties by stealing the session ID and impersonating as the authorized user. In a TCP session hijacking, the intruder takes control of the TCP session once it is successfully established between the two authorized users. Session hijacking requires the access to the session ID, which can be obtained through several approaches such as blind guessing, man-in-the-middle approach, or session sniffing. In a TCP session, the three important parameters of an in-progress communication are IP addresses, port numbers, and the sequence numbers. The intruder tries to access these three items through different mechanisms and once successful, attacks the session.

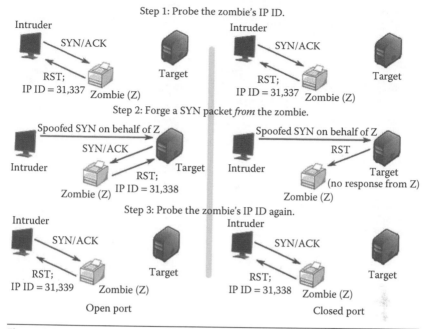

Figure 3.5 Idle scan process.

IP spoofing. Idle scan is one of the approaches categorized as spoofing approaches where the intruder hides its actual identity such as IP address or uses multiple addresses in the same attack to avoid being detected. The concept of spoofing is employed in other techniques as well such as media access control (MAC) spoofing.

File transfer protocol bounce attack. File transfer protocol (FTP) [6] bounce attack is similar to idle scan as it also involves three parties. The attack uses a vulnerability of the FTP where a client connected to an FTP server can specify any host as the recipient of the file using the PORT command. Thus, if permitted by the server, the server will attempt to create the connection with the specified destination host so that the file can be delivered. The target host in this attack is the intended recipient of the file and the response of this host to the FTP server will indicate what the intruder can achieve from this attack. For example, if the connection request is failed, this might indicate that the port is closed. A successful connection, on the other hand, indicates an open port. If the target host starts receiving the file, any kind of harmful content can be transferred through this file (Figures 3.6 and 3.7).

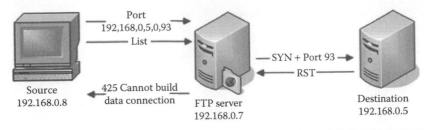

Figure 3.6   FTP bounce when port on the target is closed. Note: The syntax of the PORT command is a little strange as the address of the destination host is specified in the form of 6 comma separated decimal numbers. The first four numbers represent the IP address and can simply be used by replacing commas with dots. The last two numbers specify the port number on the destination in a format quite similar to the IP addressing. The sixth number represents the right eight bits of the port number while the fifth number represents the left eight bits of the port number; combine they make the 16-bit port number. Hence, the simple calculation to find the exact port number is to multiply the fifth number with 256 and then add to the sixth number.

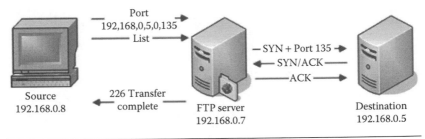

Figure 3.7   FTP bounce when port on the target is open.

3.1.4 DHCP Vulnerabilities

DHCP starvation. DHCP [7] starvation attack is a kind of spoofing, poisoning, or flooding attack, in which the intruder floods the DHCP server with lease requests by using fake MAC addresses and thus consumes all the available IP addresses. It can also be classified as a denial of service attack as the DHCP server will no longer be able to do its job, and valid users will be deprived of the IP addresses and will not be able to communicate properly.

Rogue DHCP server. The intruder introduces a rogue DHCP server into the network with the ability to respond to the DHCP discover messages. This rogue server will also be generating DHCP offers in response to the discover requests with the intention and hope that some clients might select the leases offered by it. If that happens, client can be denied of service by providing wrong network configurations. It is also possible that the intruder provides the rogue server's IP address (or of some other machine's) to the client as the gateway address, so that the client traffic should pass through the rogue server and can be analyzed for malicious purposes, thus leading to a man-in-the-middle attack (Figure 3.8).

3.1.5 ICMP Scanning

The ICMP is used by the network devices such as routers to perform error messaging. Each ICMP message carries an 8-bit type value and an

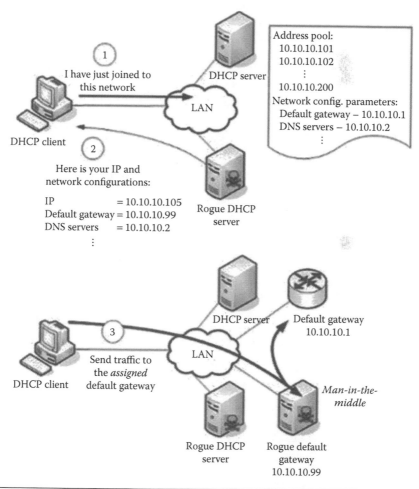

Figure 3.8   Rogue DHCP server leading to the man-in-the-middle attack.

8-bit code value, and together the two fields have an associated status/error message. For example, type 3 code 0 means destination is unreachable due to destination network unreachable. ICMP messages are used in several tools to maliciously collect information about the target networks and hosts as the ICMP requests are always responded. Some of the examples are as follows:

- Type 8 message is an echo request that is by default responded by an echo reply (Type 0) if the host is available. This technique is used to identify active devices on a network and is usually referred to as *ping scan*, due to its use in the ping utility. Ping sweep, as shown in Figure 3.9, is a enumeration technique in which ping messages are sent to a wide range of IP addresses to identify the active and non-active hosts (Figure 3.9).
- Type 13 message requests for the timestamp and thus can reveal the time zone of the target.
- Type 17 message is the network mask request and can reveal the subnetting details.

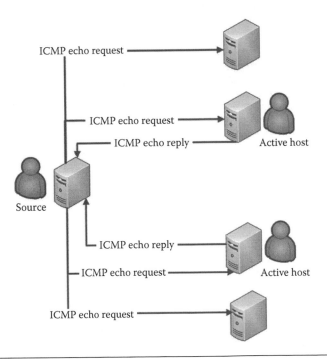

Figure 3.9 Ping sweep process.

ICMP scanning is usually not considered as a port scanning technique as the concept of ports is not valid at the level of ICMP; ports are available/addressable at the transport layer usually through TCP. It mainly helps in identifying the alive hosts on the network and thus can be categorized as a enumeration method.

UDP scan. Since UDP is a connectionless protocol, it is difficult to identify the status of the target by sending a UDP segment, as there can be multiple reasons for a no reply. However, a UDP segment sent to a port that is not associated with any application (port is closed) is responded by the target host with an ICMP Port Unreachable Message (Type 3 Code 3). Thus, a UDP segment will identify the ports that are not open.

IP scan. Several IP datagrams with varying protocol field values are transmitted to the target host. The assumption is that the target will reply with an ICMP destination protocol unreachable packet (Type 3 Code 2) for the protocols that are not supported by the host. This way the intruder can identify if the host is supporting any other transport protocols, in addition to the usual TCP and UDP.

3.1.6 Address Resolution Protocol

The address resolution protocol (ARP) [8] is also designed to provide a public service to the hosts on the LAN, that is, mapping between the network layer addresses and the physical addresses. Due to its public behavior and lack of authentication, it is vulnerable to several attacks.

ARP scan. ARP scan is a technique used to discover active hosts on the LAN. The intruder transmits ARP request with varying IP addresses, usually all the possible addresses in the subnet range. The target host if alive will reply with the MAC address and thus all the available hosts can be identified.

ARP spoofing and poisoning. ARP does not have a mechanism where the recipient of an ARP reply can authenticate if the described mapping is correct or not. This vulnerability is used in the spoofing attack, where the intruder sends ARP replies with wrong mappings to the other hosts on the LAN or replies to the ARP requests for the other hosts with its own MAC address. Thus, the traffic meant for the actual destination will instead be sent to the intruder due to wrong ARP entry at the source. Also, it will poison the ARP cache of the hosts, switches, and routers.

3.1.7 Link Layer Vulnerabilities

Packet sniffing. The LAN standards in the IEEE 802 family are generally developed with the notion of shared medium where a host can receive all the traffic on the link to which it is attached or within its reception range in case of a wireless host. In order to avoid the overhead, the network interface card looks at the source address in the frame header and stops listening if it does not match with its own address or it is not the broadcast address. However, the IEEE 802 network interface cards are designed with the possibility of a promiscuous mode, in which the network interface card receives all the traffic on the medium. This traffic can be collected by a sniffing software to perform malicious analysis. In wireless LANs such as 802.11 or in the variations of the Ethernet where more than one hosts are in the single collision domain,* sniffing attacks are always possible.

If an Ethernet is switched, that is, each host is connected to a separate port, and the switch filters the traffic on each port according to the MAC address of the host connected to that port, sniffing using the promiscuous mode is not possible due to the fact that now each port is a separate collision domain. However, this does not guarantee that sniffing is not possible at all. ARP poisoning or spoofing is one approach that can be used to sniff traffic in case of a switched Ethernet.

Ethernet switches have MAC tables or filter tables or content addressable memory tables to store the association of a MAC address with one of its port numbers, that is, what is the MAC address of the host connected on port X. It is not necessary to preconfigure the MAC table; rather, switches are designed to work in a plug-and-play fashion. In the beginning, the MAC table is empty, but when a frame is received on some port, an entry is created in the MAC table for that port with the source address of the frame as the host connected on that port.

---

* Two or more hosts are considered to be in the same collision domain if their frames can collide with each other when transmitted at the same time.

The MAC table is continuously maintained using this approach. When there is a frame to forward, the switch looks for the destination MAC address in the MAC table to identify the port on which it is connected. If an entry is found, the frame is exclusively forwarded on that port; otherwise, it is broadcasted on all the ports, except on the port on which this frame is received. Figure 3.10 provides a step-by-step example of this process.

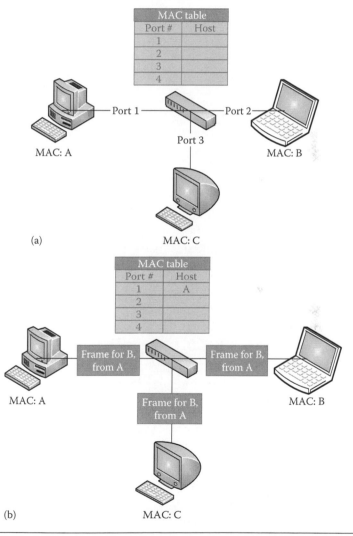

Figure 3.10   (a) Ethernet switching, in the beginning MAC table is empty. (b) A frame from A to B, new entry for A in the MAC table; frame will be forwarded on all the ports (except the port on which it is received) as there is no MAC entry for the destination B.   (*Continued*)

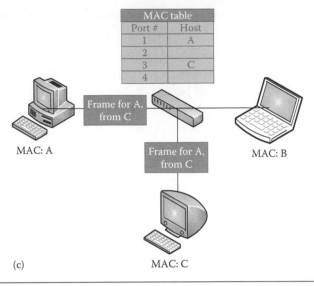

(c)

Figure 3.10 (Continued)   (c) A frame from C to A, new entry for C in the MAC table, forwarded only on the port to which A is attached.

Since the ARP packets travel as Ethernet frames, switches use them to maintain their MAC tables. In case of an ARP poisoning or spoofing attack, the switch will insert wrong mapping entries in its MAC table, which will make it possible for the intruder to sniff packets destined for other hosts.

MAC flooding. MAC flooding is another technique to confuse the Ethernet switches and make them stop filtering the frames. This attack exploits the fact that switches have a limited amount of memory to store MAC tables. When there is not sufficient memory to store new entries, most of the switches are configured to broadcast messages, so that the LAN connectivity should not be affected, referred to as the *fail open mode.* Thus, the whole LAN will become one single collision domain and packet sniffing will be possible.

In the MAC flooding attack, the intruder floods the switch with frames and every frame has a different fake MAC address. The switch as a result keeps on entering new entries into its MAC table for these new MAC addresses and eventually enters into the fail open mode.

MAC Spoofing. MAC spoofing, that is, using a different address than the one burnt in the network interface card, is permitted on most of the hardware. Intruders use this approach quite often to present themselves on the network as authorized users. Certainly, this attack requires that the intruder first use some technique to identify some valid MAC addresses on the network that can be later used for the spoofing purpose.

3.1.8 DNS Vulnerabilities

Domain name system (DNS) is an important service on the Internet where DNS servers keep mappings between the Internet domain names and host IP addresses associated with those domain names. DNS servers are implemented in a hierarchical fashion with a group of root DNS servers on the top, top-level domain servers at the second layer, and the authoritative DNS servers at the third level. DNS is a publicly accessible service to facilitate access to the Internet and its services. Due to this fact, DNS is vulnerable just like the other public services on the Internet.

Intranet DNS spoofing. Using the sniffing techniques, the intruder sniffs for DNS request message generated on the LAN. Since the DNS messages are not encrypted, anyone can look into the request content once a message is captured. The intruder then spoofs the requesting host by generating a DNS reply with wrong information. The wrong DNS information means the requested Internet addresses will be mapped to wrong hosts/IPs that can belong to some fake sites created by the intruder to capture messages sent by the attacked/victim hosts.

A common approach to capture the DNS requests is to poison the gateway/router using the ARP poisoning, so that it has an invalid DNS server entry. Thus, the router will be redirecting all the DNS requests to the intruder, assuming it as the designated local DNS server.

Internet or remote DNS spoofing. In remote DNS spoofing, the target of the intruder is any client on the Internet that can be spoofed. Thus, the approach is different as now there is not one single router to be poisoned. Such an attack is possible with the help of Trojans that are used to change the DNS settings of the victim. Once that is achieved, all the DNS requests of the victim will be sent to the fake DNS server assigned by the intruder. The consequences will be the same as in the Intranet DNS spoofing.

With the help of the Trojans, the intruder can also change the proxy server settings of the victim, so that all the traffic that is sent by the victim to the proxy server should go to the fake host.

DNS cache poisoning. Local DNS servers are maintained in the organizational networks as a cache to limit the outgoing DNS traffic and reduce the delays. These caches store the historically learnt DNS mappings and for a similar request, a response is provided by the cache. The intruder can poison this cache by adding wrong entries or changing existing entries.

3.2 Operating System Vulnerabilities

Operating systems (OSs) are softwares designed by humans and like protocols may have vulnerabilities that can be exploited by the intruders. The world of OSs is very different from the networks and the degree of interoperability is not very common. Thus, an attack can only be effective if it is designed precisely according to the nature of some OS. Unlike networks, where the identification of the protocol can be easily performed by looking at the content of the packet, determining the kind of OS requires deeper analysis and more aggressive techniques.

3.2.1 OS Fingerprinting

OS fingerprinting or OS banner grabbing is a technique used to identify the OS being used on a remote host. There are several ways through which OS fingerprinting can be performed.

TCP/IP implementation. The configuration of certain parameters in the protocols such as TCP and IP are left up to the implementation and unfortunately different OSs have their trademark implementations. An analysis of these configurations in the packets received from a target host can help the intruder in identifying the OS running on that host. In Table 3.1, a

Table 3.1 Commonly Used TCP/IP Parameters by Different Operating Systems

OPERATING SYSTEM	IP INITIAL TTL	TCP WINDOW SIZE
Linux (kernel 2.4 and 2.6)	64	5840
Google's customized Linux	64	5720
FreeBSD	64	65535
Windows XP	128	65535
Windows 7, Vista, and Server 2008	128	8192
Cisco Router (IOS 12.4)	255	4128

list of initial TTL values and Window sizes used by different OSs is provided. The scanning techniques we have discussed in Section 3.1, can be used to capture the response of the target and then the values of the two fields can be compared to identify the type of the OS. Other parameters and flags such as TCP initial sequence number and IP identification numbers can also be used to reveal the OS.

Furthermore, we have stated during our discussion on the network scanning that certain implementations of the TCP respond in a different way when an unusual protocol operation is observed. For example, the TCP RST segment in response to Xmas and null scan is only possible in the case of Berkeley Software Distribution (BSD) implementation. Similarly, the ICMP echo scanning is applicable to the BSD implementation as only these OS respond sent to the ICMP echo requests sent to the broadcast addresses.

Application Layer Protocols. HTTP, SMTP, and other application layer protocols in their message banners include the information about the OS and thus reveal the identity. The *server* and *user agent* header fields in the HTTP are prime examples of such banner grabbing.

3.2.2 Windows Platform

There are several protocols, application programming interfaces (APIs), and tools specifically used on Windows platform to maliciously attack a Windows system such as Network Basic Input and Output system (NetBIOS) and PsTools.

NetBIOS enumeration. NetBIOS is an API used on Windows platform to access LAN resources. The *nbtstat* command provided in the Windows reveals important information about the remote machines on the LAN and shared resources.

PsTools. This resource kit has several command-line tools that help to administer Windows systems. They can be also used by the intruders to collect the information about the remote and local systems.

Microsoft authentication. Microsoft LAN Manager (LM) and Microsoft Windows NT LAN Manager are proprietary protocols used by Microsoft products to perform challenge/response authentication. These protocols store passwords in the form of hashes calculated through a sequence of steps that divides the 14-character long password into two halves and process them separately to create an 8-byte hash for each part. The earlier version LM has an interesting flaw that if the password is less than or just about seven characters in length, then the second part of the hash is always 0xAAD3B435B51404EE. This can easily reveal to the intruder that the actual password length was seven characters or less.

NTFS stream manipulation. The NTFS file system on Windows platform has two data streams associated with each file stored on an NTFS volume. The first stream stores the security descriptor, while the second stream stores the data within the file. Alternate data stream (ADS) is another type of named data stream that can be present within each NTFS file. It is any kind of data that can be attached to the file but is actually not in the file. The master file table of the partition maintains a list of all the data streams associated with a file and their physical location; ADS is attached to the file through the file table.

The purpose of ADS in Windows is to provide a hidden stream that contains metadata for the file such as attributes, word count, author name, and access and modification time of the files. However, ADS can be used to fork data into existing files without changing or altering their functionality, size, or display to file-browsing utilities. Thus, ADSs provide attackers with a method of hiding malicious code or programs on a compromised system and allow them to be executed without being detected.

3.2.3 UNIX/Linux Platform

Enumeration. The finger command is used for enumerating the users on the remote machine. It provides information such as user's home directory, login time, idle times, office location, and the last time they received or read mail. Similarly, there are other commands such as rpcinfo and showmount that can be used to reveal the administrative stuff.

References

1. Fielding, R., Gettys, J., Mogul, J., Frystyk, H., Masinter, L., Leach, P., and T. Berners-Lee, "Hypertext Transfer Protocol – HTTP/1.1", RFC 2616, DOI 10.17487/RFC2616, June 1999, http://www.rfc-editor.org/info/rfc2616.
2. Postel, J., Transmission Control Protocol, STD 7, RFC 793, DOI 10.17487/RFC0793, September 1981, http://www.rfc-editor.org/info/rfc793.
3. Postel, J., User Datagram Protocol, STD 6, RFC 768, DOI 10.17487/RFC0768, August 1980, http://www.rfc-editor.org/info/rfc768.
4. Postel, J., Internet Control Message Protocol, STD 5, RFC 792, DOI 10.17487/RFC0792, September 1981, http://www.rfc-editor.org/info/rfc792.
5. Klensin, J., Ed., Simple Mail Transfer Protocol, RFC 2821, DOI 10.17487/RFC2821, April 2001, http://www.rfc-editor.org/info/rfc2821.
6. Bhushan, A., File Transfer Protocol, RFC 114, DOI 10.17487/RFC0114, April 1971, http://www.rfc-editor.org/info/rfc114.
7. Droms, R., Dynamic Host Configuration Protocol, RFC 2131, DOI 10.17487/RFC2131, March 1997, http://www.rfc-editor.org/info/rfc2131.
8. Plummer, D., Ethernet Address Resolution Protocol: Or Converting Network Protocol Addresses to 48.bit Ethernet Address for Transmission on Ethernet Hardware, STD 37, RFC 826, DOI 10.17487/RFC0826, November 1982, http://www.rfc-editor.org/info/rfc826.

4

MALWARE

MOHSEN MOHAMED

In the previous chapters, we learned about computer networks, information system security, and intrusions and vulnerabilities. This information is important because the objective of this book is to give researchers and practitioners complete information about how to use honeypots and routers to collect Internet attacks. To meet this objective, researchers should have enough information about computer networks, which will help them to design a good network against the attackers. They should also have enough information about information system security, which will help them to know the most important issues in information security. Also, researchers should have sufficient information about intrusions and vulnerabilities, which will help them to know how the intrusions can exploit the vulnerabilities to compromise networks. This chapter discusses about malware; this discussion is important because we would like to collect Internet attacks (i.e., malware), so we must know the malware in detail.

The remaining chapters of this book will cover the following topics:

Chapter 5 discusses honeypots; they are used for many objectives. One of the objectives is to collect Internet attacks; here, we will show how to use this tool to collect Internet attacks.

Chapter 6 discusses security systems such as firewall, antivirus, and intrusion detection and prevention systems. The researchers should have a thorough knowledge of these systems, which will help them to filter the known attacks and to protect the production networks.

Chapter 7 discusses real designed network to collect attacks of zero-day polymorphic worms. This will provide details on how the theoretical knowledge shared in earlier chapters can be practically implemented.

4.1 Introduction

Malware is a major threat to the security of IT infrastructure of an organization and could cause huge financial loss. Thus, the protection of network and other IT resources from this threat is of extreme importance. This chapter provides an overview about malware and how we can protect our machines against them [4].

The word *malware* is short for malicious software, and it refers to any software that disrupts the normal operation of a computing device or collects sensitive information from it or gains access to systems that are not in public domain. The use of the term *malware* is limited to the bad intent, that is, if a software affects a system accidentally or unintentionally, then it would not be considered as malware. An alternate term that includes both kind of software, that is, harming the system intentionally or unintentionally is *badware*.

Malware is used to achieve malicious objectives in several ways such as to access unauthorized data/information, secretly monitor the activities of the users of a computer, harm or sabotage the system, or extort business transactions [1].

Malware are generally categorized as follows:

- Adware
- Ransomware
- Scareware
- Spyware
- Trojan horses
- Viruses
- Worms
- Other malicious programs

Malware can be in the form of active content, executable code, scripts, or other software. The usual approach of attack is to embed the malware in some other non malicious-looking software. Trojans and worms are the most active forms of malware as compared to viruses.

The following are the software that can be used to protect networks against malware [4]:

- Intrusion detection and prevention systems
- Antivirus
- Antimalware
- Firewalls

4.2 Computer Viruses

Computer viruses are small software or programs designed to affect the routine operation of a computer system as well as to spread from one computer to the other [4]. We should mention that computer viruses cannot be activated unless they are triggered by some human/user action (e.g., opening an attached file containing virus from an email will trigger the virus; if you do not open the files, the virus will not be activated and will not harm).

A computer virus can affect the system in following ways [4]:

- Corrupt or delete the data stored on the system.
- Use one of the communication means such as email applications to spread to the other computers.
- Corrupt the hard disk in a way that the system cannot operate normally; for example, if the boot sector of the disk is erased then the system cannot load the operating system.
- Corrupt or delete data on your computer.
- Use your email program to spread itself to other computers.
- Erase everything on your hard disk.

Computer viruses [1] are usually spread in the following ways:

- They can be attached to the email messages or instant messaging messages.
- They can be disguised as attachments of funny images, greeting cards, or audio and video files.
- They also spread through downloads from the Internet and can be hidden in illicit software or other programs.

There are several approaches to protect your computer from viruses. For example, keeping your computer equipped with the strong antivirus tools and their latest updates, staying informed about recent threats, running your computer as often as possible as a standard user (not as administrator), and restraining yourself from any suspicious object when you surf the Internet, download files, and open attachments.

4.3 Computer Worms

Worms are programs that can replicate itself without requiring any user intervention; for example, by sending copies of their code over the network and ensuring that it will be executed by the recipient computers. An infected computer spreads further copies of the worm and may perform other malicious activities under the effect of the worm [1–4].

4.3.1 Worm Attack

Worms exploit low-level defects in the software present on a system, also referred to as *vulnerabilities*. Vulnerabilities are quite common in software these days due to their large size, complex structure, and use of unsafe programming languages and frameworks. Several types of vulnerabilities have been discovered over the years. Buffer overflows, arithmetic overflows, memory management errors, and incorrect handling of format strings are the most common types of vulnerabilities exploited by worms. In order to infect a computer remotely, it is necessary to coerce the computer into running the worm code, and the vulnerabilities make it possible [1].

While new types of vulnerabilities can be possibly discovered in the future, the mechanisms employed by the worms to gain control of a program's execution are less likely to change significantly over time. The three common approaches used by worms to gain control of the execution of a remote program are (1) injection of malicious code into the existing code, (2) redirecting the program flow to malicious functions, that is, forcing the program to call functions that should not be called, and (3) corrupting the data used by the program.

4.3.2 Spread of Worms

Once a computer is successfully infected by a worm, it exploits that computer to spread and propagate itself to the other computers that are reachable from the affected computer. The propagation process of the worm and the forthcoming affects such as its severity, survivability, and persistence are largely dependant on how the worm selects its victims.

The trivial and classic approach is to perform a random walk on the Internet to look for possible victims. However, novel and intelligent attack models have also been emerged that produce severe damages [1–3].

Random scanning. The simplest approach used by worms to spread themselves is to perform random network scanning. The node that contains the worm or worm code randomly generates or selects a network address range to scan. It then begins to search for potential victims in that network space such as open or unsecured ports and attacks these vulnerable hosts.

Random scanning using lists. In order to improve the efficiency of the attack and propagation process, worms may use lists/ranges of network addresses produced from the public data available on the Internet about different organizations. The scanning in this way would be more precise and directed.

Island hopping. In island hopping, the worm does not scan all the addresses from the selected range; rather, it divides the range into smaller blocks and randomly scans few addresses from each block to minimize the time. Certainly, the accuracy of this approach would also be less, as the missed hosts could be vulnerable.

Directed attack. This approach includes targeting a specific network or organization due to its significance or the attackers having special interest in it. Information warfare or attacks on some popular governmental or non governmental networks are examples of directed attack.

Hit-list scanning. Hit-list scanning is more like *random scanning with the list*, as the worm has a list of possibly vulnerable nodes before hand in this technique, and scanning is performed in that range. However, as soon as the first victim is found and successfully compromised, the main worm node assigns the half of the remaining list to this new worm node and itself continues with the other half. This way the remaining workload is reduced every time a new victim is found.

4.3.3 Worm Architecture

Worm software generally has five primary components to perform its operations, which we have mentioned above [1,4].

Reconnaissance. The life cycle of a computer worm starts with the hunt for victims. The component of the software responsible for this task is usually named *reconnaissance*. The objective of this component is similar in nature to the first phase of hacking mentioned in Section 2.5.2, also called *reconnaissance*.

Attack components. Once a vulnerable host is identified, it is attacked using one or more suitable techniques, mentioned earlier. This task is usually a separate function or component of the worm software.

Communication components. Worm software also has the functions or operations or interfaces available to facilitate communication between different members of the worm network.

Command components. One important set of communication performed among the worm nodes is to issue commands to each other to get them executed at the recipient. The worm contains a suitable list of commands and interface to execute these commands for the collective attack.

Intelligence components. This component includes algorithms and intelligent techniques for efficient operation of the worm such as faster intercommunication, efficient scanning, and so on.

4.4 Worm Examples

In this section, we discuss some popular and well-known worms [1,4], including the very first worm in computer history known as *Morris*. We will describe which vulnerabilities and operating systems the worm would target, and the high speed of worms spreading in the network and infecting computers. These examples also show instances of polymorphic worms.

4.4.1 Morris

Morris was released to attack the Internet on November 2, 1988; it is, being first of its kind, a self-replicating program. *Morris worm* invaded VAX and Sun-3 computers based on Berkeley UNIX and used their resources to replicate the attack. Within hours, the worm spread across the United States, affecting thousands of computers and making many of them unusable due to its heavy computing load. The worm was designed to execute as a tiny process to keep itself unnoticeable; however, its self-replicating behavior was underestimated and that caused serious damage by spreading the worm to as many computers as possible. The computing performance of the affected machines started degrading due to the worm process running in secret, and there were multiple instances of the worm in execution, as the same computer was attacked more than once. Eventually, because of the exhaustion of memory and other processing resources, the systems failed completely.

4.4.2 Melissa

Melissa was the first major worm spread through mail and was first recognized on March 26, 1999. Later, email became the popular medium to spread worms.

Melissa contained a Microsoft Word macro virus, a type of computer viruses that use an application's own macro programming language to distribute themselves such as Microsoft Word or Excel. It spread in a semiactive manner by attacking Microsoft Word and Outlook. Whenever, a user on the affected machine attached a Microsoft Word document to an email and used Microsoft Outlook as the email client, the copy of the email is automatically sent by the Melissa to the first 50 addresses in the user's address book.

4.4.3 Sadmind

Sadmind worm created on May 8, 2001 used vulnerabilities to compromise systems and to deface Web pages. It affected the Microsoft Internet Information Services (IIS) and Sun Solaris systems, and a patch had already been released to remove the vulnerabilities targeted by Sadmind; hence, the unpatched systems become victim to the Sadmind. Sadmind made it possible to execute arbitrary code with root privileges on vulnerable Solaris systems and arbitrary commands with the privileges of the IUSR_MachineName account on vulnerable Windows systems.

4.4.4 Code Red and Code Red II

Code Red and Code Red II, released in 2001 on July 15 and August 4 respectively, exploited the vulnerability of buffer overflow bugs in

Microsoft IIS Indexing Service dynamic link library (DLL). They affected Microsoft Windows NT 4.0, with IIS 4.0 or IIS 5.0 enabled and Index Server 2.0 installed, Windows 2000, with IIS 4.0 or IIS 5.0 enabled and indexing services installed, and other systems running IIS. It is estimated that more than 250,000 hosts suffered from their attacks.

4.4.5 Nimda

Nimda or W32/Nimda or Concept Virus (CV) v.5 was released on the Internet on September 18, 2001 to attack systems running Microsoft Windows 95, 98, ME, NT, and 2000 with unpatched versions of IIS. When a system is compromised with the help of Nimda, intruders can execute arbitrary commands within the local system security context. The worm executes with the same privileges as the user who triggered it. The infected computers suffered from denial of service due to network scanning and email propagation performed by Nimda.

4.4.6 SQL Slammer

SQL Slammer or *W32.Slammer* or *Sapphire* caused varied levels of network performance degradation across the Internet on January 25, 2003. This worm affected Microsoft SQL Server 2000 and Microsoft Desktop Engine (MSDE) 2000. The worm exploited the vulnerability of stack buffer overflow in the resolution service of Microsoft SQL Server 2000 and MSDE 2000, which enables an intruder to execute arbitrary code with the same privileges as the SQL server. The victim host starts generating high volume of user datagram protocol (UDP) traffic that results in performance degradation of the other hosts on the same network or the hosts on the Internet receiving these UDP packets.

4.4.7 Blaster

Blaster was launched on August 11, 2003. It affected computers running Microsoft Windows NT 4.0, Microsoft Windows 2000, Microsoft Windows XP, and Microsoft Windows Server 2003. Blaster exploited vulnerability in the Microsoft remote procedure call interface related to a distributed component object model listening on TCP/IP port 135. The purpose of this interface was to handle the distributed component object model's object activation requests that were sent by client machines to the server. Malformed messages and their incorrect handling helped an attacker to use buffer overflow to execute arbitrary code with system privileges or cause denial of service.

4.4.8 Sasser

Sasser is a network worm that was first detected in April 2004. It exploits buffer overflow vulnerability in the Windows Local Security Authority Service Server (LSASS) attached to TCP port 445. Like other worms, the vulnerability allows a remote attacker to execute arbitrary code with system privileges.

4.4.9 Conficker

Conficker, first detected in November 2008, targets the Microsoft Windows operating system and exploits a specific vulnerability in the server service (svchost.exe), in which an already-infected computer uses a special remote procedure call request to force a buffer overflow and executes shellcode on another computer. On the source computer, the worm establishes an HTTP server listening to a port between 1,024 and 10,000; the shellcode on the target computer forces it to connect to this HTTP server to download a copy of the worm in DLL form, which is then attached to svchost.exe.

4.4.10 Allaple

Allaple worm is a network worm also designed for the Windows platform and was first detected in August 2008. Once in execution, Allaple searches local disks for HTML files and inject code into them to activate the installed version of itself. Allaple has several variants and some of them spread to other network computers by exploiting common buffer overflow vulnerabilities or by copying itself to network shares protected by weak passwords, such as SRVSVC (MS06-040), RPC-DCOM (MS04-012), PNP (MS05-039), and ASN.1 (MS04-007).

4.5 Polymorphic Worms

A polymorphic worm is a computer worm that changes its appearance or signature in every attack [1,4].

4.5.1 Polymorphic Worm Structure

Since a polymorphic worm changes itself in every attempt, we will have multiple samples of the worm different from each other to some extent. Each sample typically consists of following components:

Protocol framework: Worms need a vulnerability in the host to affect it and continue their propagation. This vulnerability is usually associated with a particular application code and an execution path in this code that can be activated by some particular type of protocol request(s).

Exploit bytes: This is indeed the attack component of the polymorphic worm, and it exploits the target vulnerability.

Worm body: These are the main instructions of the worm that are executed on the affected hosts; polymorphic worms usually have some differences in the every instance of the worm.

Polymorphic decryptor: In order to maintain its polymorphism and to be different from instance to instance, polymorphic worms usually have the worm body in encrypted form. The decryptor extracts these instructions on the affected computer, and based on the decryption logic, a different version of worm body is produced.

Others bytes: These are additional instructions that usually do not affect the successful execution of both the worm body and the exploit bytes.

4.5.2 Polymorphic Worm Analysis

From an analyst's point of view, the binary content of a polymorphic worm sample can be classified into three kinds of bytes: invariant, code, and wildcard [1].

Invariant bytes have same or fixed value in every possible instance of the worm. They can be present in any of the worm parts discussed above, and the change in their value will make the worm ineffective. In order to generate signature for a polymorphic worm, it is extremely necessary to identify the invariant bytes, as these are necessary for the success of the worm as well as present in every instance.

Code bytes include executable components of the worm such as worm body or decryption routine. Code bytes are the main polymorphic content of the worm; however, there could be some part of code bytes that is similar across the instances.

Finally, *wildcard bytes* represent part of the worm that can have any value and this variation has no effect on the performance of the worm.

4.5.3 Signature Generation for Polymorphic Worms

The research on signature generation for polymorphic worms is in two major directions. Content-based signature generation focuses on the similarities present in the raw bytes of the different instances of a worm. On the other hand, behavior-based signatures are produced by analyzing the semantics of the worm code. Content-based signatures are advantageous, as they treat the worms as strings of bytes and do not consider any other factor. This also makes them convenient to be implemented into firewalls or network intrusion detection systems.

4.5.4 Polymorphic Worm Techniques

There are different approaches and techniques that are used in the design of polymorphic worms to achieve their polymorphism. Following is the description of some of those methods [1].

> *Self-Encryption with a Variable Key.* In this approach, the body of the worm is encrypted using a variable encryption key. Hence, the signature and the statistical characteristics of the worm raw bytes are completely diffused. The attack is launched by sending the encrypted copy of the worm, the decryption routine, and the key to the victim host. The decryption routine, extracts the original program which starts its attack once in execution. The effectiveness of this model is primarily based on the decryption routine that, if not changed often, would work as the work signature.
>
> Hence, a more sophisticated method to achieve polymorphism is to use a different decryption routine with each copy of the worm. This requires that several decryption routines are part of the worm, and out of them, one routine is randomly selected, but all the routines are encrypted together with the worm body. The number of decryption routines embedded

in the worm would directly increase its length; hence, only a limited number of routines can be added. This limitation would make it possible to use all the routines combined as worm signature once enough samples of the worm are captured.

In garbage-code insertion, a different set of garbage or useless instructions are added to each copy of the worm. For example, inserting some no operation (NOP) instructions at different places in the worm body. This will make the analysis of byte sequence more difficult due to the garbage content scattered every where in the worm body. However, the frequency of NOPs would be very different when compared with a non-malicious program, and it can be easily revealed in a statistical analysis. Anomaly-based detection systems can use this fact to detect worms. Another approach is to produce a sample of the worm minus NOPs by using some executable analysis technique and use such samples for signature generation.

The instruction substitution technique replaces an instruction sequence with an equivalent instruction sequence but with different appearance. The success of this approach depends on how many sequences are substituted in total, because the unchanged sequences will work as signature; substituting the entire code, on the other hand, would be a voluminous job.

Code transposition is a slightly modified technique that changes the order of the instructions by introducing jump instructions. However, the consequences of excessive number of jumps are similar to NOPs.

Finally, in register reassignment technique, the CPU registers used by different instructions are swapped, thus producing an equivalent code but with huge number of minor changes spread all over the code and with no statistical weakness as in NOP or jumps.

In Section 4.7, we will discuss the approaches that are used to prevent and detect the Internet worms.

4.6 Prevention and Detection of Worms

A worm is after all a program that exploits weakness in an application running on a remote host and gets the control over the execution of this vulnerable application. Therefore, the root of the problem lies within this vulnerability and to deal with it should be the first step in any prevention technique used to handle the worm. However, there is a large number of legacy programs in wide practice that cannot be modified or replaced overnight to eliminate the system vulnerabilities. Furthermore, there are vulnerabilities that are not discovered yet, and no one knows their amount. This leads us to the conclusion that prevention alone would never make the IT systems secure and detection is also equally essential [4].

Worm attacks can be prevented in two different ways: by preventing the vulnerability exploited by the worm or by controlling the exploitation of the vulnerability [1].

4.6.1 Prevention of Vulnerabilities

Secure programming languages and practices: Good programming practices and designing protocols and software in secure manner is the most effective way to reduce vulnerabilities and can resolve majority of the issues. Human errors, carelessness, and flawed assumptions are possible in the code of best and most careful programmers. C is the most commonly used language to design critical applications due to its several technical advantages over the other languages; however, because of its loose control over human errors, it is often vulnerable to buffer overflows. Thus, more secure programming and execution environments are extremely essential. Some help is available at the moment through the following [4]:

1. *Static analysis* tools
2. *Run-time checking*
3. A combination of both of the above
4. Safe languages

Secure execution environments: A secure execution environment can also ensure that no vulnerabilities will be exploited. For example, maintaining the memory integrity by using memory accesses with assertions will provide secure execution.

4.6.2 Prevention of Exploits

Unfortunately, there is no tool that comprehensively eliminates vulnerabilities of a software. Furthermore, the use of such tools is difficult and cost in terms of performance degradation that does not suits the economics of the production environment. Therefore, vendors keep on selling software with vulnerabilities to keep the attackers busy in making exploits. On top of that there are legacy system, as we mentioned earlier, that are in practice and difficult to be corrected. Preventing exploits is thus more convenient than preventing vulnerabilities. There are multiple dimensions of this prevention strategy [1]:

1. *Access control (OS dimension)*: It has always been considered the job of the operating system (OS) to control unauthorized access to system resources or contents of the file system and securely maintain access boundaries in multiuser environments. This purpose is usually achieved with the help of access control matrix and list that specify the nature of the relationship of each user with every resource of the system.

2. *Firewalls and IPS (network dimension)*: The attacks from the out of the organization can also be deterred by filtering the incoming traffic based on some rules and policies. Usually performed at the border gateways of networks, it can also be implemented at the network layer of the network protocol stack on individual machines. For example, never accept any TCP connection from a particular IP address. Another example is to drop connections with packet contents matching to a certain pattern. Filtering of traffic based on IP addresses is usually performed by firewalls that maintain a list of good and bad addresses. On the other hand, intrusion prevention systems based on signatures are used to filter traffic with unwanted patterns. There is another class of closely related software called *intrusion detection systems (IDSs)*, described in Section 4.7.

3. *Deterrents (legal dimension)*: Several technical and legal measures have been taken to stop the attacks on the computer systems. Enactment and enforcement of laws in combination with building up of audit trails on computers (to record evidence) is also helping in securing the IT systems primarily in countries with strict implementation of laws.

4.7 Intrusion Detection Systems

The research community has proposed and built IDSs to defend against Internet worms (and other attacks) [1,4]. Intrusion detection is the process of monitoring computers or networks for unauthorized entrance, activity, or file modification. IDSs can also be used to monitor network traffic, thereby detecting if a system is being targeted by a network attack such as a denial-of-service attack.

There are two basic types of intrusion detection: *host-based* and *network-based*. *Host-based* IDSs examine data held on individual computers that serve as hosts, while *network-based* IDSs examine data exchanged between computers.

There are two basic techniques used to detect intruders: *anomaly detection* and *misuse detection* (signature detection). *Anomaly detection* is designed to uncover abnormal patterns of behavior; the IDS establishes a baseline of normal usage patterns, and anything that widely deviates from it gets flagged as a possible intrusion. Although these systems can detect previously unknown attacks, they have high false positives when the normal activities are diverse and unpredictable. *Misuse detection*, which is commonly called *signature detection*, uses specifically known patterns of unauthorized behavior to predict and detect subsequent similar attempts. These specific patterns are called *signatures*. They can detect the known worms but will fail on the new types.

Most deployed worm-detection systems are signature-based, which belongs to the misuse detection category. They look for specific byte sequences (called *attack signatures*) that are known to appear in the attack traffic. The signatures are manually identified by human experts through careful analysis of the byte sequence from captured attack traffic. A good signature should be one that consistently shows up in attack traffic but rarely appears in normal traffic.

4.8 Firewalls

A firewall is a system designed to prevent unauthorized access to or from a private network. Firewalls can be implemented in both hardware and software, or a combination of both. Firewalls are frequently used to prevent unauthorized Internet users from accessing private networks connected to the Internet, especially intranets. All messages entering or leaving the intranet pass through the firewall, which examines each message and blocks those that do not meet the specified security criteria [1,4].

There are several types of firewall techniques; some of them are as follows:

- *Packet filter*: It looks at each packet entering or leaving the network and accepts or rejects it based on user-defined rules. Packet filtering is fairly effective and transparent to users, but it is difficult to configure. In addition, it is susceptible to IP spoofing.
- *Application gateway*: It applies security mechanisms to specific applications, such as FTP and Telnet servers. This is very effective, but can impose performance degradation.
- *Circuit-level gateway*: It applies security mechanisms when a TCP or a UDP connection is established. Once the connection has been made, packets can flow between the hosts without further checking.
- *Proxy server*: It intercepts all messages entering and leaving the network. The proxy server effectively hides the true network addresses.

References

1. M.M.Z.E. Mohammed, and A.-S.K. Pathan. *Automatic Defense against Zero-Day Polymorphic Worms in Communication Networks*, CRC Press, Boca Raton, FL, 2013.
2. M. Erbschloe, *Trojans, Worms, and Spyware: A Computer Security Professional's Guide to Malicious Code*, Elsevier, Burlington, MA, 2005.
3. S.G. Cheetancheri, *Collaborative Defense against Zero-Day and Polymorphic Worms: Detection, Response and an Evaluation Framework*, PhD thesis, University of California, Davis, CA, 2007, http://www.cs.ucdavis.edu/research/tech-reports/2007/CSE-2007-38.pdf.
4. M.M.Z.E. Mohammed and A.-S. K. Pathan. Automatic Defense against Zero-day Polymorphic Worms in Communication Networks, ISBN 9781466557277, CRC Press, Taylor & Francis Group, Boca Raton, FL, 2013.

5

A THEORETICAL GUIDE TO HONEYPOTS

MOHSEN MOHAMED

5.1 Honeypot Concepts

5.1.1 Introduction to Honeypots

It would be best to first define honeypot, and then talk about its history, which we deem to be an appropriate sequence of reading and understanding relevant critical information.

There are many definitions of honeypot [1,20]. In other words, there is no clearly standardized definition. Different researchers may have their own definitions of what a honeypot is. This situation has created a great deal of confusions and miscommunication. Some think that it is a tool for deception, whereas others consider it as a weapon to lure the hackers, and still others believe that it is simply another intrusion detection tool. Some believe a honeypot should emulate vulnerabilities; others see it as simply a jail. There are also some who view honeypots as controlled production systems that attackers can break into. These various viewpoints have caused a barrier to realize the true value of honeypots.

The formal definition of honeypot given by Lance Spitzner [1, p. 58] is: "A honeypot is a security resource whose value lies in being probed, attacked, or compromised."

We will now ask a series of questions to give explanations about honeypot's definition. First of all, why do we need to make a honeypot?

- We need honeypot to collect information about who is trying to compromise our system. How? The honeypot has tools that can keep traces of the source and destinations.
- Honeypot can provide us with the information about which tools and tactics have been used by the attacker to compromise

our system. Such information can be found in the techniques that have been used inside a honeypot such as firewall logs, intrusion detection systems (IDSs), and system logs. By getting this information, we can avoid such attacks in the future. How? By improving our system against these known attacks. This point (i.e., collecting information about tools and tactics) is considered as the most important goal of a honeypot. Because, anyone likes to make his system as complex as possible, so that it becomes more difficult for the attackers to compromise the system.

- By using honeypot, we can get zero-day attacks (unknown attacks). We should mention that most of the honeypot users are researchers, because honeypot provides them with extensive information about various attacks and their patterns. There are other people as well who make honeypots for other goals like finding solution for the attack in a company, or simply as a test, or for a demonstration of the concept, and so on.

An interesting fact about honeypot is that there is no value of a honeypot if it is not attacked by the attacker! This is because, to capture information about the attacker, the honeypot must be compromised. Otherwise, it has no utility as it cannot provide the required information. This point explains why we need a honeypot. Then we can ask another question that is, how can we apply a honeypot to get attacked [20]? There are several ways:

1. First, we should put a honeypot in our real network as real machines or as software in a device.
2. We should separate honeypot from other machines in the network using firewalls, routers, or other defense mechanisms. Why should we make such separation between honeypot and other machines? To safeguard other machines from the attackers.
3. If we need to improve our defense systems, then in the honeypot, we should use the same defense systems that we are using in the others protected machines. Using the same defense systems in honeypot helps us to know how the attackers can compromise these defense systems, so that we can improve them. For example, if we want to discover zero-day attacks, we should

use an updated IDPS, antivirus, and add supporting defense mechanisms. Because, these defense systems can filter out the known attacks, and then just unknown attack(s) will compromise our honeypot (which is our expectation). Therefore, we can reduce the heavy loads for our honeypot.

4. Based on need, we can use weak defense systems in the honeypot or may not use any defense system at all, if we would like to trace an attacker and get information about how it causes damage. For example, if a government wants to trace who will try to compromise their systems, then they can use a honeypot with weak defense systems or no defensive mechanism at all. Therefore, the attacker will be lured and can easily compromise the government systems. Then, the government can trace this attacker. We should note that in this case, the attacker can at least guess it as a honeypot, because if a device with weak defense systems is setup, especially in a government institution, it is highly likely that it is a honeypot. The attackers are not stupid. Hence, such trap may not always work to entice the attackers, when it comes to government institution's machines/computers.

5. We should inform all the people in an organization when we setup a honeypot, so that they do not try to access it. Therefore, anything going out or coming into the honeypot should be considered as attacks. After a considerable amount of time, we can go to the honeypot and check what it has captured. Also, in real time, we can see what exactly is happening in the honeypot.

As should be apparent from these descriptions, honeypots are different than most security tools. Most of the security technologies used today are designed to address specific problems. For example, firewall is a technology that protects your organization by controlling what traffic can flow where. They are used as an access control tool. Firewalls are most commonly deployed around an organization's perimeter to block unauthorized activity. Network IDSs are designed to detect attacks by monitoring either system or network activity.

Honeypots are different because they are not limited to solving a single, specific problem. Instead, honeypots are a highly flexible tool that can be applied to a variety of different situations. This is why the definition of honeypot may at first seem vague, because they can be used to achieve so many different goals and can come in a variety of different forms. For example, honeypots can be used to deter attacks, a goal shared with firewalls. Honeypots also can be used to detect attacks, similar to the functionality of an IDS. Honeypots can be used to capture and analyze automated attacks, such as worms, or act as early indication and warning sensors. Honeypots also have the capability to analyze the activities of the blackhat community, capturing the keystrokes or conversations of attackers. How you use honeypots is up to you. It depends on what you are trying to achieve. In Chapter 6, we will go into far greater details on the different goals you can accomplish with a honeypot. However, all possible manifestations share one common feature: their value lies in being probed, attacked, or compromised [20].

It is important to note that honeypots do not contain valuable data. Instead, they contain some kind of fake data. Therefore, honeypots are the security resources that have no production value; no person or resource should be communicating with them. As such, any activity sent their way is a *suspect* by nature. Any traffic sent to the honeypot is most likely a probe, scan, or attack. Any traffic initiated by the honeypot means the system has most likely been compromised and the attacker is making outbound connections.

Let us give a practical example to complete the understanding of the definition of honeypot. Let us consider that there is a house with three rooms. We assume that this house is targeted by the attackers. The house owner needs to know who the attacker is and how he compromises the house defense systems (i.e., doors locks, money storages, and window grills). The house owner has put all his valuable things in first two rooms, and he has set inside the third room a camera (hidden), and another camera (hidden) in the front of the room to monitor the attacker(s). The other defense systems used for the third room are as same as the defense systems used in the first two rooms, but the third room does not contain any valuable thing. In this scenario, when attacker breaks in or comes to the third room, the camera would capture all the attacker activities. So, in this case, the third room is working as the same as a honeypot does, because this room gives free movement option for the attacker but records all his moves [20].

5.1.2 History of Honeypots

In this section, we present a brief history of honeypots [1,20].

- 1990/1991—First public works documenting honeypot concepts: Clifford Stoll's *The Cuckoo's Egg* and Bill Cheswick's *An Evening With Berferd*.
- 1997—Version 0.1 of Fred Cohen's Deception Toolkit was released, one of the first honeypot solutions available to the security community [2,3].
- 1998—Development began on CyberCop Sting, one of the first commercial honeypots sold to the public. CyberCop Sting introduces the concept of multiple, virtual systems bound to a single honeypot.
- 1998—Marty Roesch and General Telephone and Electric Corporation (GTE) Internetworking begin development on a honeypot solution that eventually becomes NetFacade. This work also begins the concept of Snort [1,4].
- 1998—BackOfficer Friendly (BOF) is released—a free, simple-to-use Windows-based honeypot.
- 1999—Formation of the Honeynet Project and publication of the *Know Your Enemy* series of papers. This work helped to increase awareness and validated the value of honeypots and honeypot technologies [1,5].
- 2000/2001—Use of honeypots to capture and study worm activity. More organizations adopting honeypots for both detecting attacks and doing research on new threats.
- 2002—A honeypot is used to detect and capture in the wild, a new and unknown attack, specifically the *Solaris dtspcd* exploit.

Early publications. Surprisingly little, if any, material can be found before 1990 concerning honeypot concepts. The first resource was a book written by Clifford Stoll titled *The Cuckoo's Egg* [2]. The second is the whitepaper *An Evening with Berferd in Which a Cracker Is Lured, Endured, and Studied* [3], by the security icon Bill Cheswick. This does not mean that honeypots were not invented until 1990; they were undoubtedly developed and used by a variety of organizations well before that time. A great deal of research and deployment occurred within military, government, and commercial organizations, but very little of it was public knowledge before 1990.

In *The Cuckoo's Egg*, Clifford Stoll discusses a series of true events that occurred over a 10-month period in 1986 and 1987. Stoll was an astronomer at Lawrence Berkeley Lab who worked with and helped administer a variety of computer systems used by the astronomer community. A 75-cent accounting error led him to discover that an attacker, code named *Hunter* had infiltrated into one of his systems. Instead of disabling the attacker's accounts and locking him out of the system, Stoll decided to allow the attacker to stay on his system. His motives were to learn more about the attacker and hunt him down. Over the following months, he attempted to discover the attacker's identity while at the same time protecting the various government and military computers the attacker was targeting. Stoll's computers were not honeypots; they were production systems used by the academic and research communities. However, he used the compromised systems to track the attacker in a manner very similar to the concept of honeypots and honeypot technologies. Stoll's book is not technical; it reads more like a Tom Clancy spy novel. What makes the book unique and important for the history of honeypots are the concepts Stoll discusses in it.

The most fascinating thing in the book is Stoll's approach to gaining information without the attacker realizing it. For example, he creates a bogus directory on the compromised system called SDINET, for strategic defense initiative network. He wanted to create material that would attract the attention of the attacker. He then filled the directory with a variety of interesting-sounding files. The goal was to waste the attacker's time by compelling him to look through a lot of files. The more time he spent on the system, the more time authorities had to track down the attacker. Stoll also included documents with different values. By observing which particular documents the attacker copied, he could identify the attacker's motives. For example, Stoll provided documents that included those that appeared to have financial value and those that had government secrets. The attacker bypassed the financial documents and focused on materials about national security. This indicated that the attacker's motives were not financial gain but access to highly secret documents [20].

Bill Cheswick's paper *An Evening with Berferd in Which a Cracker Is Lured, Endured, and Studied* was released in 1990. This paper is more technical than *The Cuckoo's Egg*. It was written by security professionals for the security community. Like *The Cuckoo's Egg*, everything in Cheswick's paper is nonfiction. However, unlike the book, Cheswick builds a system that he wants to be compromised—which should be the first documented case of a true honeypot. In the paper, he discusses not only how the honeypot was built and used, but how a Dutch hacker was studied as he attacked and compromised a variety of systems.

Cheswick initially built a system with several vulnerabilities (including Sendmail) to determine what threats existed and how they operated. His goal was not to capture someone specific, but rather to learn what threatening activity was happening on his networks and systems.

Cheswick's paper explains not only the different methodologies he used in building his system (he never called it a honeypot) but also how these methodologies were used. In addition to a variety of services that appeared vulnerable, he created a controlled environment called a *jail*, which contained the activities of the attacker. He takes us step by step how an intruder (called Berferd) attempts to infiltrate the system and what Cheswick was able to learn from the attacker. We see how Berferd infiltrated a system using a Sendmail vulnerability and then gained control of the system. Cheswick describes the advantages and disadvantages of his approach. (This paper is on the CD-ROM that accompanies this book.)

Both Stoll's book and Cheswick's paper are good-read documents. However, none of the resources describes how to design and deploy honeypots in detail. And neither provides a precise definition of honeypots or explores the value of honeypot technologies.

Early products. The first public honeypot solution, called *deception toolkit (DTK)* [6], was developed by Fred Cohen. Version 0.1 was released in November 1997, seven years after *The Cuckoo's Egg* and *An Evening with Berferd in Which a Cracker Is Lured, Endured, and Studied.* DTK is one of the first free honeypot solutions one could download, install, and try out on his own. It is a collection of Perl scripts and C code that is compiled and installed on a Unix system. DTK is similar to Bill Cheswick's Berferd system in that it emulates a variety of known Unix vulnerabilities. When attacked, these emulated vulnerabilities log the attacker's behavior and actions and reveal information about the attacker. The goal of DTK is not only to gain information but also to deceive the attacker and psychologically confuse him. DTK introduced honeypot solutions to the security community.

Following DTK, in 1998, development began on the first commercial honeypot product, CyberCop Sting. This honeypot had several features different from DTK. First, it ran on Windows NT systems and not Unix. Second, it could emulate different systems at the same time, specifically a Cisco router, a Solaris server, and an NT system.

Thus, CyberCop Sting could emulate an entire network, with each system having its own unique services devoted to the operating system (OS) it was emulating. It would be possible for an attacker to scan a network and find a variety of Cisco, Solaris, and NT systems. The attacker could then Telnet to the Cisco router and could get a banner saying the system was Cisco, FTP to the Solaris server and get a banner saying the system was Solaris, or make an HTTP connection to the NT server. Even the emulated IP stacks were modified to replicate the proper OS. This way if active fingerprinting measures were used, such as Nmap [7], the detected OS would reflect the services for that IP address. The multiple honeypot images created by a single CyberCop Sting installation greatly increased the chance of the honeypots being found and attacked. This improved detection of and alerting to the attacker's activity.

For its time and development, CyberCop Sting was a cutting-edge and advanced honeypot. Also, it was easy to install, configure, and maintain, making it accessible to a large part of the security community. However, as a commercial product, it never really took off and has now been discontinued. Since its demise, several excellent commercial honeypot products have been released, including NetSec's Specter [8] and Recourse's Mantrap [9], both of which we will discuss in detail later in the book.

In 1998, Marty Roesch, while working at GTE Internetworking, began working on a honeypot solution for a large government client. Roesch and his colleagues developed a honeypot system that would simulate an entire class C network, up to 254 systems, using a single host to create the entire network. Up to seven different types of OSs could be emulated with a variety of services. Although the resulting commercial product, NetFacade [5], has seen little public exposure, an important side benefit of this honeypot solution is that Roesch also developed a network-based debugging tool, which eventually led to his open source IDS, Snort [10].

The year 1998 also saw the release of BOF, a Windows- and Unix-based honeypot developed by Marcus Ranum and released by Network Flight Recorder. What made BOF unique is that it was free, extremely easy to use, and could run on any Windows-based desktop system. All you had to do was download the tool, install it on your system, and you instantly have your own personal honeypot. Though limited in its capabilities, BOF was many people's first introduction to the concepts of honeypot technologies.

In 1999, the Honeynet Project was formed [11]. As a nonprofit research group of 30 security professionals, this group is dedicated to researching the blackhat community and sharing what they learned. Their primary tool for learning is the honeynet, an advanced type of honeypot. Over several years, the Honeynet Project demonstrated the capabilities and value of honeypots, specifically honeynets, for detecting and learning about attacks and the attackers themselves. All of the group's research methods, specifically how they designed and deployed honeypots, were publicly documented and released for the security community in a series of papers known as *Know Your Enemy*. In 2001, they released the book *Know Your Enemy* [6] that documented their research works and findings. This helped develop the awareness, credibility, and value of honeypots.

Recent history: Honeypots in action. During 2000 and 2001, there was a sudden growth in both Unix- and Windows-based worms. These worms proved to be extremely effective. Their ability to exponentially spread across the Internet astounded the Internet community. One of the challenges that various security organizations faced was obtaining a copy of the worm for analysis and understanding how it worked. Obtaining copies of the worm from compromised production systems was difficult because of data pollution or, as in the case of the Code Red worm [12], because the worms only resided in the system's memory. Honeypots proved themselves as a powerful solution in quickly capturing these worms, once again proving their value to the security community.

One example was the capture and analysis of the Leaves worm by Incidents.org. On June 19, 2001, a sudden rise of scans for the Sub7 Trojan was detected. Sub7 was a Trojan that took over Windows systems, giving an attacker total remote control of the system. The Trojan listened on the default port 27374. The attacker controlled the compromised system by connecting to this port with special client software. A team of security experts from Incidents.org attempted to find the reason for the activity.

On June 21, Johannes Ullrich of the SANS Institute deployed a honeypot he had developed to emulate a Windows system infected with the Sub7 Trojan. Within minutes, this honeypot captured an attack, giving the Incidents.org team the ability to analyze it. They discovered that a worm was pretending to be a Sub7 client and attempting to infect systems already infected by the Sub7 Trojan. This saved the attacker from the trouble of hacking into systems, since the systems were already attacked and compromised. Matt Fearnow and the Incidents.org team were able to do a full analysis of the worm, which was eventually identified as the W32/Leaves worm, and forwarded the critical information to the National Infrastructure Protection Center. Other organizations also began using honeypots for capturing worms for analysis, such as Ryan Russel at SecurityFocus.com for analysis of the CodeRed II worm. These incidents again helped develop awareness of the value of honeypots within the security community and security research.

The first recorded instance involving honeypot technologies in capturing an unknown exploit occurred on January 8, 2002. A Solaris honeypot captured a *dtspcd* exploit, an attack never seen before. On November 12, 2001, the Computer Emergency Response Team (CERT) Coordination Center, a security research organization, released an advisory for the Common Desktop Environment Subprocess Control Service [13], or, more specifically, *dtspcd*. The security community was aware that the service was vulnerable. An attacker could theoretically remotely attack and gain access to any Unix system running the *dtspcd* service. However, no actual exploit was known, and it was believed that there was no exploit being used in the wild. When a honeypot was used to detect and capture a *dtspcd* attack, it confirmed that exploit code did exist and was being used by the blackhat community. CERT was able to release an advisory [14] based on this information, warning the security community that the vulnerability was now being actively attacked and exploited. This demonstrated the value of honeypots in not only capturing known attacks, such as worms, but also detecting and capturing unknown attacks.

5.1.3 Types of Honeypots

There are mainly two types of honeypots [20]:

1. Production honeypots
2. Research honeypots

The concept of these types comes from Marty Roesch, developer of Snort. It evolved during his work and research at GTE Internetworking. Production honeypots protect an organization, while research honeypots are used for experimentation and research.

Production honeypots are easy to use, capture only limited information, and are used primarily by companies or corporations. These honeypots are placed inside the production network with other production servers by an organization to improve their overall state of security. They add value to the security of a specific organization and help mitigate risk. Normally, production honeypots give less information about the attacks or attackers than research honeypots do.

As we mentioned above, production honeypots usually are easier to build and deploy than research honeypots because they require less functionality. Production honeypots are relatively simple and generally have less risk. One of the disadvantages of the production honeypots is that they generally give us less information about the attacks or the attackers than research honeypots do. We may learn about which systems the attackers are coming from or what exploits they launch, but we will most likely not learn how they communicate among each other or how they develop their tools.

Research honeypots are often very complex to deploy. The main goals of the research honeypots are to gather extensive information about the motives and tactics of the Blackhat community targeting different networks. It should be mentioned that research honeypots do not add direct value to a specific organization; instead, they are used to research the threats that the organizations face and to learn how to better protect against those threats. Research honeypots are complex to deploy and maintain, capture extensive information, and are used primarily by research, military, or government organizations.

To get extensive information about the attackers, we need to use research honeypots; there is no other alternative. These honeypots give attackers real OSs and applications to interact. This help us to potentially learn who the attackers are, how they communicate, or how they develop or acquire their tools, but we should mention that the research honeypots have great risks as well, and require more time and effort to administer. In fact, research honeypots could potentially reduce the security of an organization, since they require extensive resources and maintenance efforts.

5.2 Types of Threats

A honeypot is a kind of security solution. Therefore, it is better to explain what the problem is, that is the attacker. By understanding who our threat is and how he operates, we can easily understand the solution better, which is the concept of honeypot [20].

5.2.1 Script Kiddies and Advanced Blackhat Attacks

There are two types of attackers: script kiddies and advanced blackhat. It does not matter if these threats are coming from the outside, such as the Internet, or from the inside, such as a disgruntled employee. Most threats tend to fall into one of these two categories.

Script kiddies. These types of attackers usually depend on scripted attacks. Sometimes, these attackers have certain requirements, such as hacking systems with a fast connection to the Internet or a large hard drive for storing files. In general, however, all they care about are numbers. They tend to be less sophisticated, but they are far more numerous, representing the vast majority of probes, scans, and attacks you see today.

To compromise a device using script kiddies is very simple, and the attacker only needs to follow a number of steps to reach its intended goal. Without script kiddies, the task is much more complicated and may only be performed by experts. For example, steps would be as follows:

- First, an attacker has to identify a vulnerability within an OS or application. This is not an easy task. It requires extensive knowledge of how OSs work, such as memory management, kernel mechanisms, and file systems' functionality. To identify vulnerabilities in an application, an attacker would have to learn how an application is operated and interacted with both the input and output of information. It could take days, weeks, or even months to identify vulnerabilities.
- However, after a vulnerability is identified, an attacker would have to develop a tool to exploit it. This requires extensive coding skills, potentially in several different computer programming languages.

- After the exploit is developed, the attacker has to find vulnerable systems. Often, one scanning tool is used to find systems that are accessible on the Internet, using such functionality as an ICMP ping or a full TCP connection. These tools are used to develop a database of systems that are accessible. Then the attacker has to determine what services existed on the reachable systems—that is, what was actually running on the targets. Furthermore, the attacker has to determine if any of these services were vulnerable.
- The next step would be launching the exploit against the victim, hacking into and gaining control of the system. Finally, various other tools (often called *rootkits*) should be used to take over and maintain control of a compromised system.

Each of these steps just described requires the development of a unique tool, and using all those tools takes a lot of time and resources. Once the attack is launched, the tools are often manually operated, requiring a great deal of work from an experienced attacker.

The above-mentioned steps are too difficult and require very skilled attackers with plenty of experience, which was not a common case. Unfortunately, today the story is too different. With almost no technical skills or knowledge, anyone can simply download tools from the Internet that can do all the works for them. Sometimes, these tools combine all of the activities that we have just described, into a fully automated weapon that only needs to be pointed at certain systems, or even at an entire network. This is as simple as just clicking a button or pressing a key on the keyboard! An attacker simply downloads these tools, follows the instructions, launches the attacks, and happily hacks his way into hundreds or even thousands of systems. These tools are rapidly spreading across the Internet, giving access to thousands of attackers, who may do such tasks just for fun. What used to be a highly complex development process is now extremely simple!

Attackers can download the automated tools from a variety of resources or exchange them with their friends. Internet relay chat (IRC) and the World Wide Web enabled blackhats to instantly share new attack tools around the world. Then, they simply learn the command-line syntax for the tool. For attackers, who are unfamiliar with command-line syntax, a variety of tools have been designed for Windows with point-and-click capabilities. Some of the exploits even come with well-written, step-by-step instructions.

Advanced blackhat. This type of attacker focuses on targets of choice, may want to compromise a specific system or systems of high value. These individuals are most likely highly experienced and knowledgeable attackers. Their attack is usually financially or nationally motivated, such as state-sponsored terrorism. They have a specific target they want to compromise, and they focus only on that one. Though less common and fewer in number, these attackers are far more dangerous due to their advanced skill level. Not only can they penetrate highly secured systems, their actions are difficult to detect and trace. Advanced blackhats make little *noise* when attacking systems, and they excel at covering their tracks. Even if you have been successfully attacked by such a skilled blackhat, you may never even be aware of it.

While script kiddies and automated attacks represent the largest percentage of attackers, the smaller, more dangerous percentage of attackers are the skilled ones that do not want anyone to know about their existence. These advanced blackhats do not release their tools. They only attack and compromise systems of high value (i.e., systems of choice). When these attackers are successful, they do not tell the world about it. Instead, they silently infiltrate organizations, collecting information, users' accounts, and access to critical resources. Often, organizations have no idea that they have been compromised. Advanced attackers can spend months, even years, within a compromised organization without anyone finding out.

These attackers are interested in a variety of targets. It could be an online banking system, where the attacker is after the database containing millions of credit card information. It could be a case of corporate espionage, where the attacker is attempting to infiltrate a car manufacturer and obtain research designs of future cars. Or it can be as sinister as a foreign government attempting to access highly confidential government secrets, potentially compromising the security of a country.

These individuals are highly trained and experienced and they are far more difficult to detect than script kiddies. Even after they have successfully penetrated an organization, they will take advanced steps to ensure that their presence or activity cannot be detected. Very little is known about these attackers. Unlike unskilled attackers, advanced blackhats do not share the same tools or techniques. Each one tends to develop his own skills, methods, and tool sets specialized for specific activities. As such, when the tools and methods of one advanced attacker are discovered, the information gained may not apply to other advanced blackhats.

We should mention that every computer connected to the Internet is exposed to a great danger. This danger may cost you all your life; for example, what would happen if an attacker uses your hard drive to store all of the stolen credit card information that he has collected? If the competent authorities for credit cards prosecute thieves, track the attacker traces, and find that the credit card information is in your computer, what will you do? It may happen that the amount of money that was stolen from the credit cards is too much. In such an embarrassing case, how can you deny the charge against you? Therefore, everyone should take care about this great issue and try to make his computer as much secure as possible.

5.2.2 Attackers' Motivations

Understanding the motivation of the attackers will help us to understand threats better. The following attacks will help for understanding why an attacker would target and attempt to compromise a system [20].

Denial of service attack. Denial of service attacks are those designed to take out the computer systems or networks of a victim. This is commonly done by flooding the intended target (such as a Web server) with a barrage of network traffic. The more traffic that is thrown at a victim, the more effective the attack is. Attackers will often compromise hundreds, if not thousands, of systems to be used for attacks. The more computers they own, the more traffic they can launch at a target. Many blackhats use denial of service attacks to take out other blackhats. One example is IRC wars, where one individual attempts to knock out another individual from an IRC channel, using denial of service attacks [15].

Internet bots. Robots (BOTs) are automated robots that act on behalf of an individual in a preprogrammed fashion. They are most commonly used to maintain control of IRC. The more computers one hacks into, the more BOTs one can launch, and the more one can control specific IRC channels. Using many BOTs protects individuals from losing control of an IRC from denial of service attacks.

Phishing. Phishing is a way of attempting to acquire information (and sometimes, indirectly, money) such as usernames, passwords, and credit card details by masquerading as a trustworthy entity in an electronic communication. Communications purporting to be from popular social websites, auction sites, online payment processors, or IT administrators is commonly used to lure the unsuspecting public. Phishing is typically carried out by email spoofing or instant messaging, and it often directs users to enter details at a fake website whose look and feel are almost identical to the legitimate one. Phishing is an example of social engineering techniques used to deceive users, and exploit the poor usability of current web security technologies. Attempts to deal with the growing number of reported phishing incidents include legislation, user training, public awareness, and technical security measures [16].

5.3 Value of Honeypots

We know now from all the above discussions that there is no specific definition of what a honeypot is. Therefore, the value of a honeypot depends on what your problem is. Or, why you need to build honeypots? The answer of these questions will highlight the value of honeypots. Therefore, the value of honeypots basically depends on your goals.

There are advantages and disadvantages of the honeypots, which affect their value. In this section, we show the advantages and disadvantages of them. Moreover, we will present the differences between production and research honeypots and their respective roles [20].

5.3.1 *Advantages of Honeypots*

There are many advantages of using honeypots, but we will focus on some of them [1,20].

- *Data value*: One of the challenges the security community faces is gaining value from data. Organizations collect vast amounts of data every day, including firewall logs, system logs, and intrusion detection alerts. The sheer amount of information can be overwhelming, making it extremely difficult to derive any value from the data. Honeypots, on the other hand, collect very little data, but what they do collect is normally of high value. The honeypot concept of no expected production activity dramatically reduces the noise level. Instead of logging gigabytes of data every day, most honeypots collect several megabytes of data per day, if even that much. Any data that is logged is most likely a scan, probe, or attack—information of high value.

  Honeypots can give you the precise information you need in a quick and easy-to-understand format. This makes analysis much easier and reaction time much quicker. For example, the Honeynet Project, a group researching honeypots, collects on average less then 1MB of data per day. Even though this is a very small amount of data, it contains primarily malicious activities. These data can then be used for statistical modeling, trend analysis, detecting attacks, or even analyzing attackers. This is similar to a microscope effect. Whatever data you capture is placed under a microscope for detailed scrutiny.

- *Resources*: Another challenge most security mechanisms face is resource limitations, or even resource exhaustion. Resource exhaustion is when a security resource can no longer continue to function because its resources are overwhelmed. For example, a firewall may fail because its connections table is full, it has run out of resources, or it can no longer monitor connections. This forces the firewall to block all connections instead of just blocking unauthorized activity. An IDS may have too much network activity to monitor, perhaps hundreds of megabytes of data per second. When this happens, the IDS sensor's buffers become full, and it begins dropping packets.

Its resources have been exhausted, and it can no longer effectively monitor network activity, potentially missing attacks. Another example is centralized log servers. They may not be able to collect all the events from remote systems, potentially dropping and failing to log critical events.

Because they capture and monitor little activity, honeypots typically do not have problems of resource exhaustion. As a point of contrast, most IDS sensors have difficulty monitoring networks that have gigabits speed. The speed and volume of the traffic are simply too great for the sensor to analyze every packet. As a result, traffic is dropped and potential attacks are missed. A honeypot deployed on the same network does not share this problem. It only captures activities directed at itself, so the system is not overwhelmed by the traffic. Where the IDS sensor may fail because of resource exhaustion, the honeypot is not likely to have a problem. A side benefit of the limited resource requirements of a honeypot is that you do not have to invest a great deal of money in hardware for it. Honeypots, in contrast to many security mechanisms such as firewalls or IDS sensors, do not require the latest cutting-edge technology, vast amounts of RAM or chip speed, or large disk drives. You can use leftover computers found in your organization or that old laptop your boss no longer wants. This means that not only can a honeypot be deployed on your gigabit network but also it can be a relatively cheap computer.

- *Simplicity*: It is the biggest single advantage of honeypots. There are no fancy algorithms to develop, no signature databases to maintain, and no rulebases to misconfigure. You just take the honeypot, drop it somewhere in your organization, and sit back and wait. While some honeypots, especially research honeypots, can be more complex, they all operate on the same simple premise: if somebody or someone connects to the honeypot, check it out. As experienced security professionals will tell you, the simpler the concept, the more reliable it is. With complexity come misconfigurations, breakdowns, and failures.
- *Fewer false positives*: We mentioned earlier that any interaction with the honeypots will be considered as suspicious. Moreover, when all people in an organization are informed that there is a

honeypot set up in the organization (i.e., some devices are acting as honeypots), nobody will try to access them.

- *Do not require known attack signatures, unlike IDS*: honeypots do not require known attack signature to detect suspicious activities. All activities in honeypots will be stored as suspicious.

5.3.2 Disadvantages of Honeypots

While it is true that the honeypots have great advantages, they also have several disadvantages [1,20]. A critical point to remember is that honeypots do not replace any security mechanisms; they only work with and enhance your overall security architecture. Let us see now some of the significant disadvantages:

- *Only monitor interactions made directly with the honeypot*: This is considered as the greatest disadvantage of honeypots. They only see what activity is directed against them. If an attacker breaks into your network and attacks a variety of systems, your honeypot will be unaware of the activity unless it is attacked directly. If the attacker has identified your honeypot for what it is, he can avoid that system and infiltrate your organization, with the honeypot never knowing something bad had happened! As noted earlier, honeypots have a microscope effect on the value of the data you collect, enabling you to focus closely on data of known value. However, like a microscope, the honeypot's very limited field of view can exclude events happening all around it.
- *Risk*: honeypots can be used by expert attackers to attack other systems. Therefore, they can be even great threats for your network.
- *Fingerprinting*: Another disadvantage found, especially in many commercial versions, is fingerprinting. Fingerprinting is when an attacker can identify the true identity of a honeypot because it has certain expected characteristics or behaviors. For example, a honeypot may emulate a Web server. Whenever an attacker connects to this specific type of honeypot, the Web server responds by sending a common error message

using standard hypertext markup language (HTML). This is the exact response we would expect from any Web server. However, if the honeypot has a weakness in it and misspells one of the HTML commands, such as spelling the word *length* as *legnht*, then this misspelling becomes a fingerprint for the honeypot. This is because any attacker can quickly identify such types of mistakes in the Web server emulation. Also, an incorrectly implemented honeypot can identify itself. For example, a honeypot may be designed to emulate an NT IIS Web server, but it also has certain characteristics that identify it as a Unix Solaris server. These contradictory identities can act as a signature for a honeypot.

If a blackhat identifies an organization using a honeypot on its internal networks, he could spoof the identity of other production systems and attack the honeypot. The honeypot would detect these spoofed attacks, and falsely alert administrators that a production system is attacking it, sending the organization on a wild goose chase. Meanwhile, in the midst of all the confusions, an attacker could focus on real attacks.

Fingerprinting is an even greater risk for research honeypots. A system designed to gain intelligence can be devastated if detected. An attacker can feed bad information to a research honeypot as opposed to avoiding detection. This bad information would then lead the security community to make incorrect conclusions about the blackhat community.

Though these disadvantages seem to be diminishing the value of honeypots, some organizations might want to use them positively to scare away or confuse attackers. Once a honeypot is attacked, it can identify itself and then warn the attacker in hopes of scaring him off. However, in most situations, organizations do not want their honeypots to be detected.

5.3.3 Roles of Honeypots in Network Security

We have discussed the advantages and disadvantages of the honeypots. So, to see what the greatest value of the honeypots could be, we must apply them to security. We may analyze how they add value to security and reduce an organization's overall risk.

The security is broken into three categories by Bruce Schneier in *Secrets and Lies* [17]: prevention, detection, and response. Here, we will discuss how honeypots can or cannot add value to each one of them.

> *Prevention.* In network security, prevention means keeping the bad guy out (i.e., preventing the bad guy from entering your network). Honeypots add a little value to prevention. Moreover, we know that honeypots can be used by the attackers to attack other systems in your organizations. The good news is that there are many methods that can be used by the honeypots to prevent the attackers from entering your organization. When attackers know that an organization has applied honeypots, they will worry about being detected and also they will waste time and resources attacking the honeypots. This method that we discussed earlier is known as prevention by deception or deterrence. The deception concept is to make attackers waste time and resources attacking honeypots, as opposed to attacking production systems. The deterrence concept is that if attackers know there are honeypots in an organization, they may be scared off. Perhaps they will not want to be detected or they will not want to waste their time or resources.
>
> We should mention that deception and deterrence fail to prevent the most common of the attacks, especially targets-of-opportunity. This is because, *targets-of-opportunity* attackers use automated tools to compromise as many systems as possible. These attackers do not spend time analyzing the systems they target. Deception or deterrence will not prevent these attacks because there is no conscious individual to deter or deceive. Finally, we can say that there is no real prevention by honeypots or a limited prevention can be provided by them.
>
> *Detection.* Detection means the act of monitoring, detecting, and alerting unauthorized activity. In Chapter 3, we have explained what the main difference between the detection and prevention is, and we also gave real-life examples. In addition to those concepts, prevention means to prevent unauthorized activities from entering your organization; but in case of detection, unauthorized activities can enter your organization

and the system sends alert in real-time to the administrators. Consequently, the administrators will check whether these activities are authorized or not. If they are unauthorized, then the administrators will deny them or purge them out.

The security community has designed several technologies for doing detection tasks; one of them is an IDS, for example. IDS is a great security solution that is designed to detect unauthorized activities in the network or on individual machines.

After these descriptions about detection, one question comes forward, that is, Do honeypots add value in detecting unauthorized or suspicious activity? The answer is Yes! honeypots add a great value in detection, which we will explore now.

There are mainly three common challenges of detection environment, which are as follows:

- False positives
- False negatives
- Data aggregation

False positives happen when the IDS falsely alert suspicious or malicious activity, typically because of flawed traffic modeling or weak rules/signatures/anomalies specified. False negatives are when system fails to detect an attack. The third challenge is data aggregation, centrally collecting all the data used for detection, and then corroborating that data into valuable information.

A single false positive is not a problem. The problem occurs when a system sends too many false positives (i.e., hundreds or even thousands of times a day). Therefore, too many false positives are a big problem, because the administrator should take care of all these false positives to check whether they are truly false positives or not. This adds to the burden of tasks of an administrator as we know that a person in that role has too many tasks to perform each day, including taking care of the IDS. If an IDS has a huge number of false positives, an administrator is supposed to give most of his time for this issue, and ignore all the other issues. Often, some people say that an IDS is good if it has a few false positives and they seem not to care about the danger of false negatives. Our view in this matter is that both false positives and false negatives are equally crucial for an organization. Because, a successful false negative will make a big problem in an organization such as information theft, network delay, and system down. Again, the false positives have a great problem that can occupy an administrator and drain him out.

It is well understood that there is not a single man-made system in the world that is 100% perfect. But, our goal is to design and develop any system as flawless as we can to the best of our abilities. A perfect system needs Godly inputs and supports, which would be free from any error, which is not applicable for human beings. Therefore, a good IDS also should have a few false positives and false negatives.

The third challenge is data aggregation as mentioned before. Modern technology is extremely effective at capturing extensive amounts of data. NIDS, system logs, application logs—all of these resources are very good at capturing and generating gigabytes of data. The challenge is how to aggregate all these data, so that they have value in detecting and confirming an attack. New technologies are constantly being devised to pull all these data together to create value, to potentially detect attacks. At the same time, new technologies are being developed that can generate more new forms of data. So, here the problem is that the technology is advancing too rapidly, and the solutions for aggregating data cannot keep up with the pace of data production.

To make a good environment for detection, we must address the above three challenges. The honeypots can address these challenges in style! Let us see how [20].

- *False positives*: Most honeypots have no production traffic, nor will it run any legitimate production services. Therefore, there is little activity to generate false positives.
- *False negatives*: Honeypots address false negatives because they are not easily evaded or defeated by new exploits. Moreover, as we know that there is little or no production activity within the honeypots, they reduce false negatives by capturing absolutely everything that enters and leaves

the system. This means that all the activities that are captured are most likely the suspects.

- *Data aggregation*: Honeypots address this issue by capturing high value data. They usually generate only several megabytes of data a day, most of which are of high value. Moreover, honeypots can capture zero-day attacks (i.e., unknown attacks), which are not detected by other security tools. This makes them extremely handy for use in network systems.

One example of using a honeypot for detection would be its deployment within a DMZ, often called the *demilitarized zone*. This is a network of untrusted systems normally used to provide services to the Internet, such as email or Web server. These are usually the systems at great risk, since anyone on the Internet can initiate a connection to them, so they are highly likely to be attacked and potentially compromised. Detection of such activity is critical. The problem is that such attacks are difficult to detect because there are so many production activities going on. All of this traffic can generate a significant amount of false positives. Administrators may quickly ignore alerts generated by traffic within the DMZ. Also, because of the large amount of traffic generated, data aggregation becomes a challenge. However, we do not want to miss any attacks, specifically false negatives. Hence, such implementation is often welcome.

Response. Once an attack is detected, we need the ability to respond to this attack. Honeypot can help protect an organization in such response event. One of the greatest challenges that the organizations face today is how to respond to an attack. There is often little information regarding the attacker(s), how they got in, or how much damage they have already done. In an attack situation, detailed information about the attacker's activities is critical. The main problem to attack response is that often the compromised system is a production system and is running essential services. Hence, it is difficult to shut it down or take it offline. Even if the system is taken offline, the logs and data entries are so much that it can be difficult to determine what normal day-to-day activities are and what the attacker's activities are.

Honeypots can help address both problems. Honeypots make an excellent incident response tool, as they can quickly and easily be taken offline for a full forensic analysis, without impacting day-to-day production operations. Moreover, the only activity a honeypot captures is unauthorized or malicious activity (as already mentioned). This makes hacked honeypots much easier to analyze than hacked production systems, as any data we retrieve from a honeypot are most likely related to the attacker. The precious gift they (i.e., honeypots) provide here is quickly giving organizations some kind of in-depth information that they (i.e., organizations) need to respond to an attack effectively. Generally, high-interaction honeypots make the best solution for response.

5.4 Honeypot Types Based on Interaction Level

Level of interaction gives us a scale with which we could measure and compare honeypots. The more a honeypot can do and the more an attacker can do to a honeypot, the greater the information that can be derived from it. However, by the same token, the more an attacker can do to the honeypot, the more potential damage an attacker can incur. Based on interaction levels, honeypots fall into three categories [1,20]: low-interaction honeypots, medium interaction honeypots, and high-interaction honeypots.

5.4.1 Low-Interaction Honeypots

Low-interaction honeypots are the simplest in terms of implementation, typically are the easiest to install, configure, deploy, and maintain because of their simple design and basic functionality. These honeypots merely emulate a variety of services. Therefore, the attacker is limited to interacting with these pre-designated services. For example, a low-interaction honeypot could emulate a standard Unix server with several running services, such as Telnet and FTP. An attacker could Telnet to the honeypot, get a banner that states the OS, and perhaps obtain a login prompt. The attacker can then attempt to log in by brute-force or by guessing the passwords. The honeypot would capture and collect these attempts, but we should mention that there is no real OS for the attacker to log in to. So, the attacker's interaction is limited to login attempts!

In fact, the main function of the low-interaction honeypots is detection, specifically of unauthorized scans or unauthorized connection attempts. As we mentioned above, low-interaction honeypots offer a limited functionality, most of this can be emulated by a program. The program is simply installed on a host system and configured to offer whatever services the admin wants, and the honeypot is ready. This makes both deployment and maintenance of the honeypot easy. All that the administrator has to do is to maintain patch levels of the program and monitor any alerting mechanisms.

Low-interaction honeypots have the lowest risk, because there are no real OSs for the attacker to interact with (i.e., all of the services are emulated not real). So, these honeypots cannot be used to harm or monitor other systems. Low-interaction honeypots log only limited information and are designed to capture known activities. An attacker can detect a low-interaction honeypot by executing a command that the emulation does not support.

One of the advantages of this approach is that the activities of the attacker are naturally *sand-boxed* within the boundaries of the software running on a host OS. The honeypot can pretend to be, for example, a Solaris server, with TCP/IP stack characteristics of a Solaris system emulated to fool OS fingerprinting and services that one would expect to see on such a server running Solaris. However, because these services are incompletely implemented, exploits written to compromise a Solaris server will at best result in a simulated compromise of the honeypot. That is, if the exploit is known and handled by the honeypot, the actual host OS is not compromised. At the worst case, the exploit will fail, because the exploit is unknown, or the vulnerability is not implemented in the honeypot.

Another advantage of the low-interaction honeypot is that the attacker is also restricted from attacking other hosts from the honeypot system. This is again because the compromise of the server is emulated.

Using low-interaction honeypots has also some disadvantages, which come from the advantages! By definition, no low-interaction emulation of an OS and its services will be complete. The responses an attacker would expect for known vulnerabilities and exploits are emulated, so a low-interaction honeypot will not respond accurately to exploits we have not included in the emulated responses. The so-called zero-day exploits would fall into this category. These exploits are kept private by the attackers and it is therefore, difficult to prepare your honeypot for these kinds of exploits [18].

5.4.2 High-Interaction Honeypots

The high-interaction honeypots are so different from low-interaction honeypots in terms of implementation and collecting information. They utilize actual OSs rather than emulations. As actual OSs are used in the high-interaction honeypots, the attacker gets a more realistic experience, and we can be able to gather more information about intended attacks. This makes high-interaction honeypots very useful in situations where one wishes to capture details of vulnerabilities or exploits that are not yet known to the public. These vulnerabilities or exploits are being used only by a small number of attackers who discovered the vulnerability and wrote an exploit for it. Such exploits are known as *zero-day* exploits. It is very important to find and publicize these vulnerabilities quickly, so that system administrators can filter or work around these problems. Also vendors can develop and release software patches to fix these vulnerabilities [18].

The high-interaction honeypots are very dangerous, because the attackers can use these systems to harm other systems. So, most often high-interaction honeypots are placed within a controlled environment, such as behind a firewall. The ability to control the attacker comes not from the honeypot itself but also from the network access control device—in many cases, the firewall. The firewall allows the attacker to compromise one of the honeypots sitting behind the firewall, but it does not let the attacker use the honeypot to launch attacks back out. Such architecture is very complex to deploy and maintain, especially if you do not want the attacker to realize that he is being monitored and controlled. A great deal of work goes into building a firewall with proper rule bases.

As we have mentioned above, the high-interaction honeypots need extensive control mechanisms; these can be extremely difficult and time consuming to install and configure. To implement high-interaction honeypots, a variety of different technologies should be combined, such as firewall and IDSs. All of the technologies have to be properly customized for the high-interaction honeypot. Maintenance is also time-consuming, because we must update firewall rule bases and IDS signature databases and monitor the honeypot activity around the clock. Because of these complexities, the high-interaction honeypots have high risk. The more interaction we allow the attacker, the more that can go wrong. However, once implemented correctly, a high-interaction honeypot can give valuable insights about attackers that no other honeypot can.

5.4.3 Medium Interaction Honeypots

Medium interaction honeypots [19] try to combine the benefits of both approaches (low- and high-interaction honeypots) with regard to botnet detection and malware collection while removing their shortcomings.

The key feature of medium interaction honeypots is application layer virtualization. They do not aim at fully simulating a full operational system environment, nor do they implement all details of an application protocol. What the medium interaction honeypots do is to provide sufficient responses that known exploits wait on certain ports that will trick them into sending their payloads.

Once the payload has been received, the shellcode is extracted and analyzed somehow. The medium interaction honeypot then emulates the actions the shellcode would perform to download the malware. Therefore, the honeypot has to provide some virtual file system as well as virtual standard Windows download utilities. The honeypot can then download the malware from the serving location and store it locally or submit it somewhere else for analysis.

5.5 Overview of Five Honeypots

In this section, we present an overview of five notable honeypots [1,20]. These examples can give the readers some idea about what honeypot products are available (the open source products and the commercial versions).

5.5.1 BackOfficer Friendly

BOF was developed by Marcus Ranum and the folks at Network Flight Recorder. The BOF is commonly called as a simple, free honeypot solution. BOF is considered a low-interaction honeypot designed to run on almost any Windows system.

BOF is very simple, so anyone can install it on their system; also, it is easy to configure and requires low maintenance. Because of the fact that it is simple, its capabilities are also severely limited. It has a small set of services that simply listen on ports, with notably limited emulation capabilities.

5.5.2 Specter

Specter is developed and sold by NetSec, and it is considered as a commercially supported honeypot. Specter is also considered as a low-interaction honeypot like BOF, but it has more functionality and capabilities than BOF. In fact, Specter is not just the emulated services, but it has the ability to emulate different OSs and vulnerabilities. It also has extensive alerting and logging capabilities. Moreover, Specter is easy to deploy, simple to maintain, and is less risky as it only emulates services with limited interaction. However, compared to medium and high-interaction honeypots, it is limited in the amount of information that it can gather. Specter is primarily a production honeypot.

5.5.3 Honeyd

Honeyd is considered as an open source low-interaction honeypot. The main functions of Honeyd are to

- Detect
- Capture
- Alert suspicious activity

Honeyd was developed by Niels Provos in April 2002. It introduces several new concepts for honeypots. First, it does not monitor a single IP address for activity; instead, it monitors networks of millions of systems. When it detects probes against a system that does not exist, it dynamically assumes the identity of the victim and then interacts with the attacker, exponentially increasing the ability of the honeypots to detect and capture attacks. It can emulate hundreds of OSs, at both the application and IP stack levels. As an open source solution,

Honeyd is a free technology, giving you full access to the source code. You can customize your own solutions or use those developed by other members of the security community. Designed for the Unix platform, Honeyd is relatively easy to install and configure, relying primarily on a command-line interface.

5.5.4 ManTrap

ManTrap is considered as a medium- to high-interaction honeypot, and it is a commercial honeypot sold by Recourse. ManTrap does not emulate any services such as BOF, Specter, and Honeyd. Instead, it takes an OS and creates up to four virtual OSs. This gives the administrator extensive control and data-capturing capabilities over the virtual OSs. Organizations can even install production applications that they want to test, such as DNS, Web servers, or even a database. These virtual OSs have almost the exact same interaction and functionality as standard production systems. Thus, a great deal can be learnt from the attacker.

ManTrap is fairly easy to deploy and maintain as a commercial product. It can also capture an incredible amount of information. Not only does ManTrap detect scans and unauthorized connections but also it can capture unknown attacks, blackhat conversations, or new vulnerabilities. However, its versatility comes at the cost of increased risk. As the honeypot has a full OS for the attacker to work with, the honeypot can be used to attack other systems and execute unauthorized activity.

One limitation of ManTrap is that it is currently limited to the Solaris OS. At the time of writing this book, versions for other OSs are under development, but they have not yet been released. As technology moves forward at great speed, the readers are suggested to seek for the latest product version. ManTrap has the flexibility to be used as either a production or research honeypot, although it is most commonly used for production purposes.

5.5.5 Honeynets

Honeynets are high-interaction honeypots. In fact, it is difficult to envisage any other honeypot solution that can offer a greater level of interaction than honeynets do. The concept of a honeynet is simple: building a network of standard production systems, just as we would find in most organizations today. Putting this network of systems behind some type of access control device (such as a firewall) and watching what happens. Attackers can probe, attack, and exploit any system within the honeynet, giving them full OSs and applications to interact with. No services are emulated, and no caged environments are created. The systems within a honeynet can be anything: a Solaris server running an Oracle database, a Windows XP server running an IIS Web server, a Cisco router, and so on. In short, the systems within a honeynet are true production systems [1,20].

The complexity of a honeynet is not in the building of the honeypots themselves (they can easily be nothing more than default installations), but rather in building the controlled network that both controls and captures all the activities that are happening to and from the honeypots. As such, honeynets are some of the most difficult honeypots to both deploy and maintain. This complexity makes honeynet as the highest-risk honeypot solution. One of the most important advantages of honeynets is that they can also capture the greatest level of information on almost any platform that may exist. Honeynets are primarily used for research purpose. Because of the incredible amount of works involved, they have little value as production honeypots.

> *Virtual honeynets.* Virtual honeynet is a solution that allows you to run everything you need on a single computer. We use the term *virtual*, because different OSs have the *appearance* to be running on their own independent computers, which are not real machines. These solutions are possible because of virtualization software that allows running multiple OSs at the same time, on the same hardware. Virtual honeynets are not a radically new technology; they simply take the concept of honeynet technologies and implement them into a single system. This implementation has its unique advantages and disadvantages over traditional honeynets [11].
>
> The advantages of virtual honeynet include reduced cost and easier management, as everything is combined into a single system. Instead of taking many computers to deploy,

with a full honeynet, you can do it with only one computer. However, this simplicity comes at a cost. First, you are restricted to choose what types of OSs you can deploy by the hardware and virtualization software. For example, most virtual honeynets are based on the Intel X86 chip, so you are restricted to OSs based on that architecture. You most likely cannot deploy an Alteon switch, VAX, or Cray computer within a Virtual honeynet. Second, virtual honeynets come with a risk. Specifically, an attacker may be able to compromise the virtualization software and take over the entire honeynet, giving them control over all the systems. Finally, there is the risk of fingerprinting. Once the bad guys have hacked the systems within your virtual honeynet, they may be able to determine what systems are running in a virtual environment.

We have broken virtual honeynets into two categories: self-contained and hybrid. Of the two, self-contained is the more common. We will first define these two different types, and then cover the different ways that virtual honeynets can be deployed.

Self-contained virtual honeynets. A self-contained virtual honeynet is an entire honeynet network condensed onto a single computer. The entire network is virtually contained on a single, physical system. A honeynet network typically consists of a firewall gateway for data control and data capture, and the honeypots within the honeynet. Some advantages of this type of Virtual honeynet(s) are as follows:

- *Portable*: Virtual honeynets can be placed on a laptop and taken anywhere. The Honeynet Project demonstrated this functionality at the Blackhat Briefings in August, 2002.
- *Plug and catch*: You can take the one box and just plug it in to any network and can be ready to catch those blackhats. This makes deployment much easier, as you are physically deploying and connecting only one system.
- *Cheap in money and space*: You only need one computer, so it cuts down on your hardware expenses. It also has a small footprint and only takes one outlet and one port! For those of us with very limited space and power, this is a life saver.

There are some disadvantages as well:

- *Single point of failure*: If something goes wrong with the hardware, the entire honeynet could be out of commission.
- *High-quality computer*: Even though a self-contained honeynet only requires one computer, it will have to be a powerful system. Depending on your setup, you may need a great deal of memory and processing power.
- *Security*: Since everything might be sharing the same hardware, there is a danger of an attacker getting at other parts of the system. Much of this depends on the virtualization software, which will be discussed in Section 5.5.5.
- *Limited software*: Since everything has to run on one box, you are limited to the software you can use. For instance, it is difficult to run Cisco IOS on an Intel chip.

Hybrid virtual honeynet. A hybrid virtual honeynet is a combination of the classic honeynet and virtualization software. Data capture, such as firewalls, and data control, such as IDS sensors and logging, is on a separate, isolated system. This isolation reduces the risk of compromise. However, all the honeypots are virtually run on a single box. The advantages to this setup are as follows [20]:

- *Secure*: As we saw with the self-contained virtual honeynets, there is a danger of an attacker getting to the other parts of the honeynet (like the firewall). With hybrid virtual honeynets, the only danger would be that the attacker accessing to the other honeypots.
- *Flexible*: You are able to use a wide variety of software and hardware for the data control and data capture elements of the Hybrid network. An example would be that you can use the OpenSnort sensor on the network, or a Cisco pix appliance. You can also run any kind of honeypot you want because you can just drop another computer on the network (in addition to your Virtual honeypot's box).

Some disadvantages are as follows:

- *Not portable*: Since the honeynet network will consist of more than one box, it makes it more difficult to move.

– *Expensive in time and space*: You will have to spend more in terms of power, space, and possibly money since there is more than one computer in the network.

Virtualization software. Hybrid virtual honeynets can allow you to leverage the flexibility of classic honeynets and let you increase the amount of honeypots by using virtualization software. Now that we have defined the two general categories of virtual honeynets, let us highlight some of the possible ways to implement a virtual honeynet. Here, we outline three different technologies that will allow you to deploy your own. Undoubtedly, there are other options, such as Bochs; however, the Honeynet Project has used and tested all three methods. No one solution is better than the other. Instead, each of them has its own unique advantages and disadvantages, it is up to you to decide which solution works best. The three options we will now cover are VMware workstation, VMware GSX server, and user-mode Linux (UML).

VMware workstation. VMware workstation is a long used and established virtualization option. It is designed for the desktop user and is available for Linux and Windows platforms. Advantages to using VMware workstation as a virtual honeynet are as follows:

1. *Wide range of OS support*: You are able to run a variety of OSs within the virtual environment (called *Guest OSs*), including Linux, Solaris, Windows, and FreeBSD honeypots.

2. *Networking options*: Workstation provides two ways to handle networking. The first is bridged, which is useful for hybrid virtual honeynet networks because it lets a honeypot use the computer's card and appear to be any other host on the honeynet network. The second option is host-only networking; this is good for self-contained virtual honeynets because you are able to better control traffic with a firewall.

3. *VMware workstation creates an image of each guest OS*: These images are simply a file, making them highly portable. This means that you can transfer them to

other computers. To restore a honeypot to its original condition, you can just copy a backup into its place.

4. *Ability to mount VMware virtual disk images*: You are able to mount a VMware image just like you would mount a drive using vmware-mount.pl.

5. *Easy to use*: VMware workstation comes with a graphical interface (both Windows and Linux) that makes installing, configuring, and running the OSs very simple.

6. *As a commercial product*: VMware workstation comes with support, upgrades, and patches.

Some disadvantages are as follows [20]:

1. *Cost*: VMware workstation costs $300 per license (price may vary over time). This might be a bit much for the hobbyist, or the unemployed student.

2. *Resource requirements*: VMware workstation must run under an X environment, and each virtual machine (VM) will need its own window. So, on top of the memory you allocate for the guest OSs, you have the overhead of the X system.

3. *Limited amount of guest OSs*: With VMware you can only run a small number of VM, ~1–4. This might make for a limited honeynet.

4. *Closed source*: Since VMware is closed source, you cannot really make any custom adjustments.

5. *Fingerprinting*: It may be possible to fingerprint the VMware software on a honeypot, especially if the *VMware tools* are installed on the systems. This could give the honeypots away to the blackhat. However, VMware workstation does have options that can make fingerprinting more difficult, such as the ability to set the MAC address for virtual interfaces.

VMware products also have some nice features, like the ability to suspend a VM. You are able to *pause* the VM, and when you take it out of suspension, all the processes go on like nothing happened. An interesting use of VMware, and other virtualization software too, is the ease and speed of bringing up VMs. Once a honeynet is compromised, and we learned as much as we can from it, we want to start over. With a virtual honeynet, all we have to do is copy files or use the undoable disk or non-persistent disk feature in VMware workstation to discard any changes made. Another feature of VMware workstation is the ability to run several networks behind the host OS. Therefore, if you only have one box, you can have your honeynet and personal computers all on the one box without worrying about data pollution on either side. If you would like to learn more about VMware and its capabilities for honeypot technology, check out Kurt Seifiried's excellent paper *honeypotting with VMware—The Basics* and Ryan Barnett's *Monitoring VMware honeypots*.

VMware GSX server. The VMware ground storm X (GSX) server is a heavy-duty version of VMware workstation. It is meant for running many higher end servers. As we will see, this is perfect for use as a honeynet. The GSX server currently runs on Linux and Windows as a host OS. If you would like to learn more about deploying virtual honeynets on GSX, check out the paper *Know Your Enemy: Learning with VMware*.

Advantages of using the GSX server are as follows:

1. *Wide range of OS support*: The GSX server supports Windows (including 95, 98, NT, 2000, XP, and .NET server), various Linux distributions, and potentially BSD and Solaris (not officially supported).

2. *Networking*: It includes all of the options that a workstation has.

3. *No X means more guest OSs*: The GSX server does not need X running in order to have VMware running. This allows you to run many more guest OSs at the same time. However, it does require that some of the X libraries be installed if the host is running Linux.

4. *Web interface*: The GSX server can be managed through a web page interface. Guest OSs can be started, paused, stopped, and created via the web page.

5. *Remote terminal*: This is one of the best features of the GSX server. Through the web page and with some VMware software, you can remotely access the guest

OSs as if you were sitting at the console. You are able to do things like remote installs and checking out the system without generating traffic on the honeynet.

6. *Ability to mount*: Virtual disk images can be created.
7. *VMware GSX server supports more host memory (up to 8GB)*: More CPUs (up to 8), and more memory per VM (2BG) than VMware workstation.
8. Includes a Perl API to manage guest OSs.
9. *Similar to workstation*: The GSX server is a supported product, including patches and upgrades.

Some disadvantages are as follows:

1. *Cost*: A GSX server license will run around $3500 (again, cost may vary over time, please check for the latest).
2. *Limited types of guest OSs*: OSs like Solaris X86 and FreeBSD are not officially supported (however, you may be able to install them). This can limit the diversity of your honeynet.
3. *Memory hog*: The GSX server recommends greater than 256 MB just to run the GSX server software. GUI-based OSs, such as Windows XP, require another 256 MB for each instance.
4. *Closed source*: Just like workstation.
5. *Fingerprinting*: It may be possible to fingerprint the VMware software on a honeypot, especially if the *VMware tools* are installed on the systems. This could expose the honeypots to the hackers. However, like workstation, there are configuration options that can reduce that risk.

VMware also makes a VMware ESX server. Instead of being just a software solution, the ESX server runs in hardware of the interface. It provides its own VM OS monitor that takes over the host hardware. This allows more granular control of resources allocated to VMs, such as CPU shares, network bandwidth shares, and disk bandwidth shares and it allows those resources to be changed dynamically. This product is even higher end than the GSX server.

Some of its features are it can support multiple processors, more concurrent VMs (up to 64 VMs), more host memory (up to 64 GB), and more memory per VM (up to 3.6 GB) than the GSX server.

User-mode Linux. UML is a special kernel module that allows you to run many virtual versions of Linux at the same time. Developed by Jeff Dike, UML gives you the ability to have multiple instances of Linux, running on the same system at the same time. It is a relatively new tool with great amounts of potential. You can learn in detail how to deploy your own UML honeynet from the paper *Know Your Enemy: Learning with User-Mode Linux.* Some advantages of using UML are as follows:

1. It is free and open source; you have access to the source code.
2. It has small footprint and fewer resource requirements. UML does not need to use X. It can also run extensive amount of systems with little memory.
3. It has the ability to create several virtual networks and even create virtual routers all inside the original virtual network.
4. It supports both bridging and networking, similar to VMware.
5. UML has the ability to log keystrokes through the guest OS kernel. The keystrokes are logged right on the host OS, so there are no issues with how to get the keystrokes off the honeypot in a stealth way.
6. UML comes with preconfigured downloadable file systems, making it fast and easy to populate your honeynet with honeypots. Like VMware, these file system images are mountable.
7. You can access UML consoles in a wide variety of ways, including through pseudoterminals, xterms, and portals on the host, which you can Telnet to. And there is always screen. Run UML inside screen, detach it, and you can log in to the host from anywhere and attach it back.

Some disadvantages are as follows:

1. It currently supports only Linux VM; however, a port to Windows is under development.
2. As a new tool, there are some bugs, documentation, and security issues.
3. There is no GUI; currently, all configurations and implementations are done at the command line.
4. As an open source tool, there is no official or commercial support.
5. Similar to VMware, it may be possible to fingerprint a UML honeynet due to the virtualization software.

5.6 Conclusion

Before concluding this chapter, it should be clarified that honeypots do not do the same functions as an IDS does. Yes, they have some similarities but from the operational point of view, they are fairly different. For example, if we would like to devise a good IDS for a network, we must collect valuable data about attacks, then analyze these attacks to generate signatures for them, then we have to use these signatures in the IDS. Honeypots, on the other hand, are good tools to collect valuable data but they are set up for being attacked by the potential attackers. A honeypot is not a usual defense mechanism meant for protecting a system, but an IDS is a core part of the defense system or strategy. Honeypots are often deployed for collecting valuable information about the attackers that could be analyzed and used for developing appropriate countermeasures, while IDS simply implements a set of rules based on which it detects whether there is any rogue entity that enters into the network and then it asks for purging it out.

References

1. L. Spitzner, *Honeypots: Tracking Hackers*, Addison-Wesley, Boston, MA, September 20, 2002.
2. C. Stoll, *The Cuckoo's Egg: Tracking a Spy through the Maze of Computer Espionage*, 1st edition, Pocket Books, New York, October 1, 2000.
3. B. Cheswick, An evening with Berferd in which a cracker is lured, endured, and studied, *Proceedings of the Winter 1992 USENIX Technical Conference*. USENIX Association, San Francisco, CA, January 20–24, 1992.

4. NetFacade honeypot, http://www22.verizon.com/fns/solutions/netsec/netsec_netfacade.html, last accessed August 11, 2012.
5. *Know your enemy*, The Honeynet Project, 2001, Addison-Wesley, Boston, MA, http://project.honeynet.org/book/, last accessed September 6, 2015.
6. Deception Toolkit, http://www.all.net/dtk/index.html, last accessed August 11, 2012.
7. Nmap, https://nmap.org/, last accessed September 6, 2015.
8. Specter honeypot, http://www.specter.com, last accessed August 11, 2012.
9. Mantrap honeypot, http://www.mantrap.com, last accessed August 11, 2012.
10. Snort, Open Source Intrusion Detection System, http://www.snort.org, last accessed August 11, 2012.
11. The Honeynet Project, http://project.honeynet.org, last accessed August 11, 2012.
12. CERT Advisory CA-2001–18, *Multiple Vulnerabilities in Several Implementations of the Lightweight Directory Access Protocol (LDAP)*, http://www.cert.org/advisories/CA-2001-18.html, last accessed August 11, 2012.
13. CERT Advisory CA-2001–31, *Buffer Overflow in CDE Subprocess Control Service*, http://www.cert.org/advisories/CA-2001-31.html, last accessed August 11, 2012.
14. CERT Advisory CA-2002–01, *Exploitation of Vulnerability in CDE Subprocess Control Service*, http://www.cert.org/advisories/CA-2002-01.html, last accessed August 11, 2012.
15. DDoS and Security Reports, http://ddos.arbornetworks.com/, last accessed August 11, 2012.
16. K.Y. Tan, *Phishing and Spamming via IM (SPIM)*, http://isc.sans.org/diary.php?storyid=1905, last accessed August 11, 2012.
17. B. Schneier, *Secrets and Lies: Digital Security in a Networked World*, 1st edition, Wiley, New York, August 14, 2000.
18. D.N. Pasman, Catching hackers using a virtual honeynet: A case study, *Proceedings of the 6th Twente Student Conference on IT*, University of Twente, Enschede, the Netherlands, February 2, 2007.
19. G. Wicherski, *Medium Interaction honeypots*, April 2006, http://citeseerx.ist.psu.edu/viewdoc/summary?doi=10.1.1.133.9431, last accessed August 11, 2012.
20. M.M.Z.E. Mohammed and A.-S. K. Pathan, Automatic Defense against Zero-day Polymorphic Worms in Communication Networks, ISBN 9781466557277, CRC Press, Taylor & Francis Group, Boca Raton, FL, 2013.

6
SECURITY SYSTEMS

MOHSEN MOHAMED

The objective of security systems is to manage and report operational information security risk in the networks.

This chapter covers the following security systems:

- Firewall
- Antivirus
- Intrusion detection and prevention systems (IDPSs)

6.1 Firewall

A firewall is a system designed to prevent unauthorized access to or from a private network. Firewalls can be implemented in both hardware and software, or a combination of both. Firewalls are frequently used to prevent unauthorized Internet users from accessing private networks connected to the Internet, especially intranets. All messages entering or leaving the intranet pass through the firewall, which examines each message and blocks those that do not meet the specified security criteria [1,20].

6.1.1 Types of Firewalls

Firewalls can be either hardware or software but the ideal firewall configuration [20] will consist of both. In addition to limiting access to your computer and network, a firewall is also useful for controlling remote access to a private network and perform it in a secure manner through appropriate authentication.

Hardware firewalls. This type of firewall can be purchased as a stand-alone product but are also typically found in broadband routers, and should be considered as an important part of your system and network setup. Most hardware firewalls will have a minimum of four network ports to connect other computers, but for larger networks, business networking firewall solutions are available.

Software firewalls. This type can be installed on your computer (like any software) and you can customize it; allowing you some control over its function and protection features. A software firewall will protect your computer from outside attempts to control or gain access to your computer.

6.1.2 Common Firewall Techniques

As we know that firewalls are used to protect both home and corporate networks. A typical firewall software or hardware device filters all information coming through the Internet to your network or computer system. There are many types of firewall techniques that will prevent potentially harmful information from getting through [1,20].

Packet filters (Stateless). If a packet matches the packet filter's set of rules, the packet filter will drop or accept it.

Stateful filters. It maintains records of all connections passing through it and can determine if a packet is either the start of a new connection, a part of an existing connection, or is an invalid packet.

Application layer. It works like a proxy and it can *understand* certain applications and protocols. It may inspect the contents of the traffic, blocking what it views as inappropriate content (i.e., websites, viruses, and vulnerabilities).

6.2 Antivirus

It is a computer software program that is used to prevent, detect, and remove malicious software. Antivirus software was originally developed to detect and remove computer viruses, hence the name. However, with the proliferation of other kinds of malware, antivirus software has started to provide protection from other computer threats. In particular, modern antivirus software can protect from malicious browser helper objects, browser hijackers, ransomware, keyloggers, backdoors, rootkits, Trojan horses, worms, malicious layered service providers (LSPs), dialers, fraudtools, adware, and spyware [1,20]. Some products also include protection from other computer threats, such as infected and malicious uniform resource locators (URLs), spam, scam and phishing attacks, online identity (privacy), online banking attacks, social engineering techniques, advanced persistent threats, botnets, and distributed denial-of-service (DDoS) attacks.

6.3 Intrusion Detection and Prevention Systems

An intrusion detection system (IDS) is a device or software application that monitors network or system activities for malicious activities or policy violations and produces reports to the administrators. So, the main function of IDS is detection by sending report to the administrators; therefore, there is no prevention task in the IDS; the prevention can be done manually by the administrators after receiving the alert from the IDS. An intrusion prevention system (IPS) is a network of security appliances that monitors network and/or system activities for malicious activity attempting to block/stop activity, and report activity. So, the main function of IPS is automatic prevention and also sending report to the administrators about the case. A combination of the IDS and IPS is called *IDPS*. Most of the organizations now use IDPS products because they offer great defense mechanisms [1,20].

Let us give two real-life examples to explain more about the main difference between the IDS and IPS.

Example 6.1

Let us consider, we have a big house, and there is a security guard to protect this house from the attackers or unwanted outsiders. The security guard is always sitting at the main entrance of the house, and the house is equipped with a warning bell, which gets activated at 1 a.m. and remains active till 8 a.m. The warning bell sends alert if anyone tries to enter the house forcefully or by illegitimate means (i.e., anyone not coming through the main entrance, which is the legal way). If the warning bell sends an alert, the security guard would go to see what exactly has happened. In fact, if the warning bell sends an alert, that may not always mean that there is an attacker trying to break in the house; it may even be someone among the members of the house (legitimate one)! If an illegal person penetrates the house and the warning bell does not send an alert, this is considered as a false negative. If the warning bell sends an alert for a legal person (by mistake), this is considered as a false positive. From this example, it is clear that the warning bell acts as an IDS exactly and the security guard is working as the network administrator. So, what are the benefits of an IDS, if it does not protect organizations from attacks automatically (i.e., just by sending the IDS alert)? The above example answers this question; that is, without the warning bell, the security guard would not be able to know that someone was trying to penetrate the house. Therefore, the network administrators would not be able to know there are some attacks that have been launched without the IDS alert. We should mention here that some types of IDSs have limited capabilities to prevent attacks from entering an organization, but in general, the main function of the IDS is detection, not prevention [20].

Example 6.2

We find in some countries that some people put a wire on the wall of their houses, which could be electrified by turning on an electrical switch. The house owner turns on the switch, say for example, from 1 a.m. to 8 a.m. to prevent an attacker/burglar from entering the house. This example is similar to that of an IPS, because this method can prevent the burglar from entering the house easily.

Combination of the above two examples can be considered as the mechanism of an IDPS. It should be noted here that we presented Example 6.2 just to give the idea of the main function of an IPS. In a real-life situation, an electrified wire like that may cause fatality, which is not supportable. The voltage level, however, could be accordingly set, so that it does the work of prevention of illegal entry to the house, not causing any severe fatality. It is of course better to avoid such mechanism to put in practice in real-life case [20].

6.3.1 Introduction

Figure 6.1 shows at a glance what this chapter will cover. The numbers shown in the figure are not the section numbers, but just to relate the items we have used those. As can be seen, first, we give an introduction about the IDPS. Then, we discuss the IDPS detection technologies: signature-based detection, anomaly-based detection, and stateful protocol analysis. Then, we give details about the IDPS components: sensors or agents, management server, database server, and console. After that, we discuss the IDPS security capabilities against

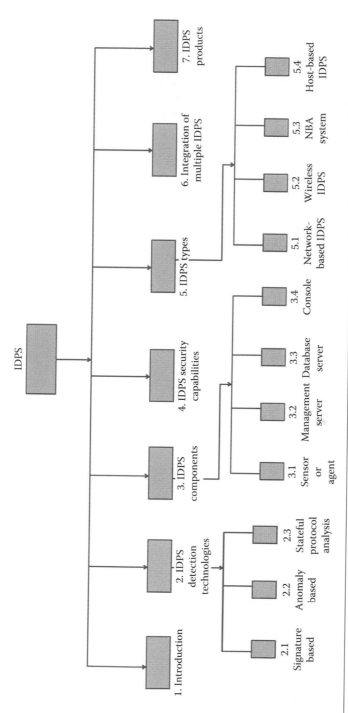

Figure 6.1 Contents of this chapter at a glance.

authorized activities. After that, we discuss the types of the IDPS technologies: network-based IDPS, wireless IDPS, network behavior analysis (NBA) system, and host-based IDPS. When referring to the types of the IDPS technologies, we mean at which level we put the IDPS product; for example, within a house, we can put the warning bell on the house wall, which is similar to the network-based IDPS; also, we can put it in any of the rooms, which is similar to the host-based IDPS. Before concluding the chapter with some examples of IDPS products, we discuss the advantages of integrating multiple IDPS technologies and integrating different IDPS products [20].

The IDSs and IPSs [2] are considered as the main defense methods against Internet worm and other types of security attacks. The main function of an IDS is to monitor the events occurring in a computer system or network and analyze them to detect unauthorized activities and consequently, alert the security administrators to take appropriate actions. On the other hand, the main function of an IPS is to identify unauthorized activities and attempt to block/stop them. IPS can be considered as relatively a bit more sophisticated system, which is put in place to block an attack from its initial trial.

To obtain a good defense performance, the security experts often combine the IDS and IPS into a single system, called *IDPS*. The main functions of the IDPSs are focused on identifying possible incidents, logging information about them, attempting to stop them, and reporting them to security administrators.

The IDPSs generally do the following tasks on observing any event [20]:

1. Record information related to observed events
2. Notify security administrators of important observed events
3. Produce reports to the security administrators

There are several IDPSs that, after recording a suspicious activity (or a threat), can also respond to it by attempting to prevent it from succeeding. There are several response techniques used by the IDPSs, involving the actions like stopping the attack itself, changing the security environment (e.g., reconfiguring a firewall), or changing the attack's content.

Organizations, banks, educational institutes, research labs, offices, or wherever computer systems are used for networking and communications, it is recommended to ensure that all IDPS components are appropriately secured. Securing IDPS components is a critical matter in many networking system because the attackers may attempt to avoid the IDPSs from detecting attacks or can try to gain access to sensitive information in the IDPSs, such as host configurations and known vulnerabilities. The IDPSs have several types of components, including the following [2,3,20]:

1. Sensors or agents
2. Management servers
3. Database servers
4. User and administrator consoles
5. Management networks

All components' operating systems and applications should be always kept updated, and all software-based IDPS components should be developed in the best intricate way possible, so that potential threats are diminished and the security protections may not be breached easily.

Specific protective actions of particular importance include creating separate accounts for each IDPS user and administrator, restricting network access to IDPS components, and ensuring that IDPS management communications are protected appropriately, such as encrypting them or transmitting them over a physically or logically separate network. Administrators should maintain the security of the IDPS components on a continuous basis, including verifying that the components are functioning as desired, monitoring the components for security issues, performing regular vulnerability assessments, responding appropriately to vulnerabilities in the IDPS components, and testing and deploying IDPS updates. Administrators should also back up configuration settings periodically and ensure before applying updates that the existing settings are not inadvertently lost.

To obtain more comprehensive and accurate detection and prevention of Internet worm and other attacks, different types of organizations need to consider using different types of IDPS technologies. There are four primary types of IDPS [2,4,20] mechanisms available today, which are as follows:

1. Network-based
2. Wireless

3. NBA-based
4. Host-based

Each of the above-mentioned mechanisms provides a different type of defense against malicious activities (i.e., the network-based mechanism can detect attacks that the host-based mechanism cannot or may not detect). For example, the network-based mechanism can detect attacks on the network level, whereas the host-based can detect attacks at the host level. To obtain a good and effective defense solution, a combination of network-based and host-based IDPS mechanisms is needed. If the organization determines that its wireless networks need additional monitoring, it can use the wireless IDPS technologies to obtain a good defense performance.

If organizations desire additional detection capabilities for denial of service (DoS) attacks, worms, and other threats, it is recommended to use the NBA technologies to achieve that goal. The organizations that plan to use multiple types of IDPS technologies or multiple products of the same type of IDPS are recommended to be aware of whether or not the IDPSs should be integrated.

There are two types of IDPS integrations. They are as follows [2,20]:

1. *Direct IDPS integration*: The process of a product feeding information to another product is called *direct IDPS integration*. Direct IDPS integration is most suitable when an organization uses multiple IDPS products from a single vendor. For example, a network-based IDPS technology perhaps uses host-based IDPS data to determine whether an attack is detected successfully by the network-based IDPS technology, and a network-based IDPS technology could give network flow information to an NBA IDPS technology. The feeding information helps in improving detection accuracy, speed up the analysis process, and help in ordering of threats according to their priorities. The main drawback of using a fully integrated solution is that a failure or compromise could affect all the IDPS technologies negatively.

2. *Indirect IDPS integration*: Indirect IDPS integration is the process when many IDP products send their data to security information and event management (SIEM) software. The main function of the SIEM software is to import information

from various security-related logs and correlate events among them. The SIEM software commonly receives copies of the logs from the logging hosts over security network channels, then it normalizes the log data into standard fields and value (known as *normalization*), and then determines related events by matching Internet protocol (IP) addresses, timestamps, usernames, and other characteristics. SIEM products can do the following tasks: identify malicious activity such as attacks and malware infections, as well as misuse and inappropriate usage of systems and networks.

SIEM software can complement IDPSs. For example, if an organization uses different IDPS technologies, the SIEM software can correlate events logged for these different IDPS technologies. The SIEM software can identify incidents that a single device cannot; also, it can collect information related to an event in a single place to make more efficient analysis. However, there is a significant limitation in the SIEM software: a delay between the time when an event begins and the time SIEM software sees the corresponding log data, since log data are often transferred in batch mode to conserve resources. Resource consumption is also limited by SIEM products transferring only some event data from the original resources.

Organizations should define the requirements that the products should meet before evaluating IDPS products. To do this task, evaluators need to understand the characteristics of the organization's system and network environments. Then, evaluators can select a compatible IDPS that can monitor the events of interest on the systems and/or networks. Evaluators should explain well the goals and objectives they wish to achieve by using an IDPS, such as stopping common attacks, identifying misconfigured wireless network devices, and detecting misuse of the organization's system and network resources. In addition, evaluators should reconsider their existing security policies, which serve as a specification for many of the features that the IDPS products need to provide. Evaluators should also understand whether or not the organization is subject to oversight or review by another organization. If so, the evaluators should determine if that oversight authority requires IDPSs or other specific system security resources. Resource constraints should also be taken into account by evaluators.

Moreover, the evaluators need to define specialized sets of requirements for the following [20]:

- Security capabilities in depth, including the methodologies that they use to identify suspicious activity
- Performance, including maximum capacity and performance features
- Management, including design and implementation (e.g., reliability, interoperability, scalability, and product security); operation and maintenance (including software updates); and training, documentation, and technical support
- Life cycle costs, both initial and maintenance costs

When an organization evaluates IDPS products, it should consider using a combination of several sources of data on the products' characteristics and capabilities. Common product data sources include test lab or real-world product testing, vendor-provided information, third-party product reviews, and previous IDPS experience from individuals within the organization and trusted individuals at other organizations. When data are received from other parties, the organization should consider the fidelity, because those are often presented without an explanation of how those were generated. There are several significant challenges in performing in-depth hands-on IDPS testing, such as the need of considerable amount of resources and lack of a standard test methodology and test suites, which often make it infeasible. However, limited IDPS testing is helpful for evaluating security requirements, performance, operation, and maintenance capabilities.

6.3.2 IDPS Detection Methods

IDPS technologies use many methods to detect attacks. The primary methods are signature-based, anomaly-based, and stateful protocol analysis. Most IDPS technologies use more than one method to provide more accurate detection. We present more details about the mentioned methods in the following sections [2,20].

> *Signature-based detection.* A signature is a pattern that corresponds to a known threat. A signature-based detection scheme monitors packets in the network and compares them against a database of signatures from known malicious

threats. This method works similar to the way most antivirus software detect malware. The main disadvantage of this kind of method is that there would always be a lag between a new threat being discovered in the wild and the signature for detecting that threat being applied to an IPS. During that lag time, the IPS would be unable to detect the new threat.

The signature-based detection method is considered as the simplest detection method because it just compares the current unit of activity, such as a packet or a log entry, to a list of signatures using string comparison operations. Another limitation that these kinds of detection technologies have is their little understanding of many network or application protocols and they cannot track and understand the state of complex communications. For example, signature-based detection methods cannot pair a request with the corresponding response, such as knowing that a request to a Web server for a particular page generated a response status code of 403 means that the server refused to accept the request (in fact, 403 error is equivalent to a blanket *NO* by the Web server—with no further discussion allowed). These methods also lack the ability to remember previous requests when processing the current request. This limitation prevents signature-based detection methods from detecting attacks that comprise multiple events if none of the events contains a clear indication of an attack [2,5,20].

Anomaly-based detection. An anomaly-based detection method monitors network traffic and compares it against an established baseline. The baseline identifies what is *normal* for that network, what sort of bandwidth is generally used, what protocols are used, what ports and devices generally connect to each other, and alert the administrator or user when traffic is detected, which is anomalous, or significantly different than the baseline.

The major advantage of anomaly-based detection methods is that they can be very effective at detecting previously unknown threats. For example, suppose that a computer becomes infected with a new type of malware. The malware could consume the computer's processing resources, send large number of emails, initiate large number of network connections, and show other behaviors that would be significantly different from the established profiles for the computer.

An initial profile is generated over a period of time (typically days, sometimes weeks) sometimes called a *training period*. There are two types of anomaly-based profiles: (1) static and (2) dynamic. Once generated, a static profile is unchanged unless the IDPS is specifically directed to generate a new profile. A dynamic profile is adjusted constantly as additional events are observed. The reality is that the systems and networks change over time, so the corresponding measures of normal behavior also change. A static profile will eventually become inaccurate; hence, it needs to be regenerated periodically. Dynamic profiles do not have this problem, but they are susceptible to evasion attempts from attackers. For example, an attacker can perform small amounts of malicious activities occasionally, then slowly increase the frequency and quantity of activities. If the rate of change is sufficiently slow, the IDPS might think the malicious activity is normal behavior and include it in its profile! Malicious activity might also be observed by an IDPS while it builds its initial profiles.

Inadvertently including malicious activity as part of a profile is a common problem with anomaly-based IDPS products. (In some cases, administrators can modify the profile to exclude activity in the profile that is known to be malicious.) To develop a good anomaly-based detection scheme, experts should study network activities well (such as the traffic rate, the number of packets for each protocol, the rate of connections, and the number of different IP addresses), then put these activities in a profile. However, there is another critical problem associated with building profiles for which it can be very challenging in some cases to make them accurate, because computing activities can be very complex. For example, if a particular maintenance activity that performs large file transfers occurs only once a month, it might not be observed during the training period; when the maintenance occurs, it is likely to be considered as a significant deviation from the profile and triggers an alert (which would be a false detection/false positive)!

An IPS's evaluation tools are false negatives and false positives. A false negative occurs when an attack or an event is either not detected by the IDS or is considered benign by the analyst. A false positive occurs when an event is picked up by the IDS and declared as an attack but actually it is not or it is benign. The main disadvantage of the anomaly-based IDPS products is that they often produce many false positives because of benign activity that deviates significantly from profiles, especially in more diverse or dynamic environments. Another noteworthy problem with the use of anomaly-based detection techniques is that it is often difficult for analysts to determine why a particular alert was generated and to validate that an alert is accurate and not a false positive, because of the complexity of events and number of events that may have caused the alert to be generated [2,6,20].

Stateful protocol analysis. Stateful protocol analysis method identifies deviations of protocol states by comparing observed events with *predetermined profiles of generally accepted definitions of benign activity.* This method, unlike anomaly-based detection (which uses host or network-specific profiles), relies on vendor-developed universal profiles that specify how particular protocols should and should not be used. The *stateful* in stateful protocol analysis means that the IDPS is capable of understanding and tracking the state of network, transport, and application protocols that have a notion of state. For example, when a user starts a file transfer protocol session, the session is initially in the unauthenticated state. Unauthenticated users should only perform a few commands in this state, such as viewing help information or providing usernames and passwords. An important part of understanding state is pairing requests with responses, so when a file transfer protocol authentication attempt occurs, the IDPS can determine if it was successful by finding the status code in the corresponding response. Once the user has authenticated successfully, the session is in the authenticated state, and users are expected to perform any of several dozen commands. Performing most of these commands while in the unauthenticated state would be considered suspicious, but in the authenticated state, performing most of them is considered benign.

Unexpected sequences of commands can be identified by the stateful protocol, such as issuing the same command repeatedly or issuing a command without first issuing a command upon which it is dependent. In addition, there is another state-tracking feature of stateful protocol analysis, that is, for protocols that perform authentication; the IDPS can keep track of the authenticator used for each session, and record the authenticator used for suspicious activity. This is helpful when investigating an incident. Some IDPSs can also use the authenticator information to define acceptable activity differently for multiple classes of users or specific users.

Stateful protocol analysis methods perform protocol analysis to detect attacks, which includes reasonableness checks for individual commands, such as minimum and maximum lengths for arguments. If a command typically has a username argument, and usernames have a maximum length of 20 characters, then an argument with a length of 1000 characters is suspicious. If the large argument contains binary data, then it is even more suspicious.

To detect unauthorized activities, stateful protocol analysis methods use protocol models, which are typically based primarily on protocol standards from software vendors and standards bodies (e.g., Internet Engineering Task Force Request for Comments). The protocol models also typically take into account variances in each protocol's implementation. Many standards are not exhaustively complete in explaining the details of the protocol, which causes variations among implementations. Also, many vendors either violate standards or add proprietary features, some of which may replace features from the standards. For proprietary protocols, complete details about the protocols are often not available, making it difficult for IDPS technologies to perform comprehensive, accurate analysis. As protocols are revised and vendors alter their protocol implementations, IDPS protocol models need to be updated to reflect those changes.

The main disadvantage of the stateful protocol analysis methods is that they are very resource-intensive because of the complexity of the analysis and the overhead involved in performing state tracking for many simultaneous sessions. Another disadvantage is that the stateful protocol analysis methods cannot detect attacks that do not violate the characteristics of generally acceptable protocol behavior, such as performing many benign actions in a short period of time to cause a DoS. Yet another problem is that the protocol model used by an IDPS might conflict with the way the protocol is implemented in particular versions of specific applications and operating systems, or how differently client and server implementations of the protocol interact [2,7].

6.3.3 IDPS Components

In this section, we mention typical components in an IDPS solution [2,12]. They are as follows:

- *Sensor or agent*: The main function of this component is to monitor and analyze activity. The term *sensor* is typically used for IDPSs that monitor networks, and the term *agent* is typically used for IDPS technologies that monitor only a single host.
- *Management server*: A management server is a device that receives information from sensors or agents and manages it. There are some management servers that perform analysis on the information received and can identify incidents that the individual sensor or agent cannot. Matching event information from multiple sensors or agents, such as finding events triggered by the same IP address is known as *correlation*. Some small IDPS deployments do not use any management servers. In larger IDPS deployments, there are often multiple management servers, sometimes in tiers.
- *Database server*: A database server is a repository for event information recorded by sensors, agents, and management servers. Many IDPSs support the use of database servers.
- *Console*: A console is a program that provides an interface for the IDPS users and administrators. Console software is typically installed on standard desktop or laptop computers. Some consoles are used for IDPS administration only, such as configuring sensors or agents and applying software updates,

whereas other consoles are used strictly for monitoring and analysis. Some IDPS consoles provide both administration and monitoring capabilities.

IDPS components can be connected with each other through regular networks or a separate network designed for security software management known as a *management network*. If a management network is used, each sensor or agent host has an additional network interface known as a *management interface* that connects to the management network, and the hosts are configured, so that they cannot pass any traffic between management interfaces and other network interfaces. The management servers, database servers, and consoles are attached to the management network only. This architecture effectively isolates the management network from the production networks, concealing the IDPS from attackers and ensuring that the IDPS has adequate bandwidth to function under adverse conditions. If an IDPS is deployed without a separate management network, a way of improving IDPS security is to create a virtual management network using a virtual local area network within the standard networks. Using a virtual local area network provides protection for IDPS communications, but not as much protection as a separate management network.

6.3.4 IDPS Security Capabilities

IDPS technologies offer extensive and accurate detection capabilities. To provide more accurate detection, IDPS products use a combination of detection techniques. The types of events detected and the typical accuracy of detection vary greatly depending on the type of IDPS technology. Most IDPSs require at least some tuning and customization to improve their detection accuracy, usability, and effectiveness. Examples of tuning and customization capabilities are as follows [2,12]:

- *Thresholds*: A threshold is a value that sets the limit between normal and abnormal behavior. Thresholds usually specify a maximum acceptable level, such as five failed connection attempts in 60 s, or 100 characters for a filename length.
- *Blacklists and whitelists*: A blacklist is a list of discrete entities, such as hosts, transmission control protocol (TCP) or user datagram protocol (UDP) port numbers, Internet control message protocol types and codes, applications, usernames,

URLs, filenames, or file extensions, that have been previously determined to be associated with malicious activity. Blacklists allow IDPSs to block activity that is highly likely to be malicious. Some IDPSs generate dynamic blacklists that are used to temporarily block recently detected threats (e.g., activity from an attacker's IP address). A whitelist is a list of discrete entities that are known to be benign. Whitelists are typically used on a granular basis, such as protocol by protocol, to reduce or ignore false positives involving known benign activity.

- *Alert settings*: Most IDPS technologies allow administrators to customize each alert type. Examples of actions that can be performed on an alert type include toggling it on or off and setting a default priority or severity level. Some products can suppress alerts if an attacker generates many alerts in a short period of time, and may also temporarily ignore all future traffic from the attacker. This is to prevent the IDPS from being overwhelmed by alerts.

- *Code viewing and editing*: Some IDPS technologies permit administrators to see some or all of the detection-related code. This is usually limited to signatures, but some technologies allow administrators to see additional code, such as programs used to perform stateful protocol analysis. Viewing the code can help analysts determine why particular alerts were generated, so they can better validate alerts and identify false positives. The ability to edit detection-related code and write a new code (e.g., new signatures) is necessary to fully customize certain types of detection capabilities.

Most IDPSs offer multiple prevention capabilities to provide more accurate detection; the specific capabilities vary by IDPS technology type. IDPSs usually allow administrators to specify the prevention capability configuration for each type of alert. This usually includes enabling or disabling prevention, as well as specifying which type of prevention capability should be used. Some IDPS technologies offer information gathering capabilities such as collecting information on hosts or networks from observed activity. Examples include identifying hosts and the operating systems, applications that they use, and identifying general characteristics of the network.

6.3.5 *Types of IDPS Technologies*

As we mentioned earlier, there are mainly four types of IDPS technologies [12]:

- Network-based IDPS
- Wireless IDPS
- NBA system
- Host-based IDPS

In this section, we present details about these IDPS technologies [12].

Network-based IDPS. Network-based IDPSs are placed at a strategic point or points within the network to monitor traffic to and from all devices in the network. A network-based IDPS monitors and analyzes all inbound and outbound traffic for particular network segments or devices to identify suspicious activity; however, doing so might create a bottleneck that would impair the overall speed of the network. The IDPS network interface cards are placed into promiscuous mode, so that they accept all packets that they see, regardless of their intended destinations. In fact, most of the IDPSs perform their analysis at the application layer, for example, hypertext transfer protocol, simple mail transfer protocol, and domain name system. They also analyze activity at the transport (e.g., TCP and UDP) and network (e.g., IPv4) layers to identify attacks at those layers and facilitate application layer analysis. Some network-based IDPSs also perform limited analysis at the hardware layer, for example, address resolution protocol.

Network-based IDPS sensors can be deployed in one of two modes: in-line or passive.

- An in-line sensor is deployed so that the traffic it monitors passes through it. Some in-line sensors are hybrid firewall/IDPS devices. The primary motivation for deploying sensors in-line is to stop attacks by blocking traffic.
- A passive sensor is deployed so that it monitors a copy of the actual traffic; no traffic passes through the sensor. Passive sensors can monitor traffic through various methods, including a switch spanning port, which can see all traffic going through the switch; a network tap, which is a

direct connection between a sensor and the physical network medium itself, such as a fiber optic cable; and an IDS load balancer, which is a device that aggregates and directs traffic to monitoring systems.

Most techniques having a sensor that prevent intrusions require that the sensor be deployed in in-line mode. Passive techniques typically provide no reliable way for a sensor to block traffic. In some cases, a passive sensor can place packets onto a network to attempt to disrupt a connection, but such methods are generally less effective than in-line methods. IP addresses are normally not assigned to the sensor network interfaces (which are used to monitor traffic), except for network interfaces that are also used for IDPS management. Operating of a sensor without IP addresses assigned to its monitoring interfaces is known as *stealth mode*. It improves the security of the sensors because it conceals them and prevents other hosts from initiating connections to them. However, attackers may be able to identify the existence of a sensor and determine which product is in use by analyzing the characteristics of its prevention actions. Such analysis might include monitoring protected networks and determining which scan patterns trigger particular responses and what values are set in certain packet header fields.

Network-based IDPS security capabilities against malicious activity. Network-based IDPSs provide extensive and broad detection capabilities. Most IDPSs use a combination of signature-based, anomaly-based, and stateful protocol analysis detection techniques. These techniques are usually tightly interwoven; for example, a stateful protocol analysis engine might parse activity into requests and responses, each of which is examined for anomalies and compared against signatures of known bad activity.

Most types of events commonly detected by network-based IDPS sensors include application, transport, and network layer reconnaissance and attacks. Many sensors can also detect unexpected application services, such as tunneled protocols, backdoors, and hosts running unauthorized applications. Also, some types of security policy violations can be detected by sensors that allow administrators to specify the characteristics of activity that should not be permitted, such as TCP or UDP port numbers, IP addresses, and website names. Some sensors can also monitor the initial negotiation conducted when establishing encrypted communications to identify client or server software that has known vulnerabilities or is misconfigured. Examples include secure shell, transport layer security, and IP security.

Network-based IDPSs are associated with high rates of false positives and false negatives. These rates can only be reduced to some extent because of the complexity of the activities being monitored. A single sensor may monitor traffic involving hundreds or thousands of internal and external hosts, which run a wide variety of frequently changing applications and operating systems. A sensor cannot understand everything it sees. Another common problem with detection accuracy is that the IDPS typically requires considerable tuning and customization to take into account the characteristics of the monitored environment. Also, security controls that alter network activity, such as firewalls and proxy servers, could cause additional difficulties for sensors by changing the characteristics of traffic.

Usually, network-based schemes can collect limited information on hosts and their network activity. Examples of these are a list of hosts on the organization's network, the operating system versions and application versions used by these hosts, and general information about network characteristics, such as the number of hops between devices. This information can be used by some IDPSs to improve detection accuracy. For example, an IDPS might allow administrators to specify the IP addresses used by the organization's Web servers, mail servers, and other common types of hosts, and also specify the types of services provided by each host (e.g., the Web server application type and version run by each Web server). This allows the IDPS to better prioritize alerts; for example, an alert for an Apache attack directed at an Apache Web server would have a higher priority than the same attack directed at a different type of Web server.

Some network-based IDPSs can also import the results of vulnerability scans and use them to determine which attacks would likely be successful, if not blocked. This allows the IDPS to make better decisions on prevention actions and prioritize alerts more accurately.

Network-based IDPS sensors offer many prevention capabilities. A passive sensor can attempt to end an existing TCP session by sending TCP reset packets to both end points, to make it appear to each end point that the other is trying to end the connection. However, this technique often cannot be performed in time to stop an attack and can only be used for TCP; other, newer prevention capabilities are more effective. In-line sensors can perform in-line firewalling, throttle bandwidth usage, and alter malicious contents. Both passive and in-line sensors can reconfigure other network security devices to block malicious activity or route it elsewhere, and some sensors can run a script or program when certain malicious activity is detected to trigger custom actions.

Network-based IDPS limitations. Although network-based IDPSs provide extensive detection capabilities, they do have some significant limitations. Attacks within encrypted traffic would not be detected by the network-based IDPSs, including virtual private network connections, hypertext transfer protocol over secure sockets layer, and secure shell sessions. To ensure that sufficient analysis is performed on payloads within encrypted traffic, IDPSs can be deployed to analyze the payloads before they are encrypted or after they have been decrypted. Examples include placing network-based IDPS sensors to monitor decrypted traffic and using host-based IDPS software to monitor activity within the source or destination host.

When a high load appears in a network, the network-based IDPSs may be unable to perform full analysis. This leads to some attacks to go undetected, especially if stateful protocol analysis methods are in use. For in-line IDPS sensors, dropping packets also causes disruptions in network availability, and delays in processing packets could cause unacceptable latency. To avoid this, some in-line IDPS sensors can recognize high load conditions and either pass certain types of traffic through the sensor without performing full analysis or drop low-priority traffic. Sensors may also provide better performance under high loads if they use specialized hardware (e.g., high-bandwidth network cards) or recompile components of their software to incorporate settings and other customizations made by administrators.

IDPS sensors can be avoided by various types of attacks. Attackers can generate large volumes of traffic, such as DDoS attacks, and other anomalous activity (e.g., unusually fragmented packets) to exhaust a sensor's resources or cause it to crash. Another attack technique, known as *blinding*, generates traffic that is likely to trigger many IDPS alerts quickly. In many cases, the blinding traffic is not intended to actually attack any target. An attacker runs the *real* attack separately at the same time as the blinding traffic, hoping that the blinding traffic will either cause the IDPS to fail in some way or cause the alerts for the real attack to go unnoticed. Many sensors can recognize common attacks against them, alert administrators to the attack, and then ignore the rest of the activities.

Wireless IDPS. A wireless IDPS monitors wireless network traffic and analyzes wireless networking protocols to identify malicious behavior. However, it cannot identify suspicious activity in the application or higher-layer network protocols (e.g., TCP and UDP) that the wireless network traffic is transferring. It is most commonly deployed within the range of an organization's wireless network to monitor it, but it can also be deployed to locations where unauthorized wireless networking could be occurring.

Because of the transmission methods, wireless network attacks differ from those on wired networks. However, the basic components involved in a wireless IDPS are the same as the network-based IDPS: consoles, database servers, management servers, and sensors. A wireless IDPS monitors the network by sampling the traffic. There are two frequency bands to monitor (2.4 and 5 GHz), and each band includes many channels. A sensor is used to monitor a channel at a time and it can switch to other channels as needed.

We should mention that most of the wireless local area networks (WLANs) use the Institute of Electrical and Electronics Engineers (IEEE) 802.11 family of WLAN standards [8]. IEEE 802.11 WLANs have two main architectural components, which are as follows:

- A station, which is a wireless end-point device (e.g., laptop computer, personal digital assistant).
- An access point, which logically connects stations with an organization's wired network infrastructure or other network.

Some WLANs also use wireless switches, which act as intermediaries between access points and the wired network. A network based on stations and access points is configured in infrastructure mode; a network that does not use an access point, in which stations connect directly to each other, is configured in an ad hoc mode. Nearly all organizational WLANs use infrastructure mode. Each access point in a WLAN has a name assigned to it called a *service set identifier*. The service set identifier allows stations to distinguish one WLAN from another.

Wireless sensors have several available forms. A dedicated sensor is usually passive, performing wireless IDPS functions but not passing traffic from source to destination. Dedicated sensors may be designed for fixed or mobile deployment, with mobile sensors used primarily for auditing and incident handling purposes (e.g., to locate rogue wireless devices). Sensor software is also available bundled with access points and wireless switches. Some vendors also have host-based wireless IDPS sensor software that can be installed on stations, such as laptops. The sensor software detects station misconfigurations and attacks within the range of the stations. The sensor software may also be able to enforce security policies on the stations, such as limiting access to wireless interfaces.

If an organization uses WLANs, it most often deploys wireless sensors to monitor the radiofrequency range of the organization's WLANs, which often includes mobile components such as laptops and personal digital assistants. Many organizations also use sensors to monitor areas of their facilities where there should be no WLAN activity, as well as channels and bands that the organization's WLANs should not use, as a way of detecting rogue devices.

Wireless IDPS security capabilities. The main advantages of wireless IDPSs include detection of attacks, misconfigurations, and policy violations at the WLAN protocol level, primarily examining IEEE 802.11 protocol communication. The major limitation of a wireless IDPS is that it does not examine communications at higher levels (e.g., IP addresses and application payloads). Some products perform only simple signature-based detection, whereas others use a combination of signature-based, anomaly-based, and stateful protocol analysis detection techniques. Most of the types of events commonly detected by wireless IDPS sensors include unauthorized WLANs and WLAN devices and poorly secured WLAN devices (e.g., misconfigured WLAN settings). Additionally, the wireless IDPSs can detect unusual WLAN usage patterns, which could indicate a device compromise or unauthorized use of the WLAN, and the use of wireless network scanners. Other types of attacks such as DoS conditions, including logical attacks (e.g., overloading access points with large numbers of messages) and physical attacks (e.g., emitting electromagnetic energy on the WLAN's frequencies to make the WLAN unusable) can also be detected by wireless IDPSs. Some wireless IDPSs can also detect a WLAN device that attempts to spoof the identity of another device.

Another significant advantage is that most wireless IDPS sensors can identify the physical location of a wireless device by using triangulation—estimating the device's approximate distance from multiple sensors from the strength of the device's signal received by each sensor, then calculating the physical location at which the device would be, the estimated distance from each sensor. Handheld IDPS sensors can also be used to pinpoint a device's location, particularly if fixed sensors do not offer triangulation capabilities or if the device is moving.

Wireless IDPS overcome the other types of IDPS by providing more accurate prevention; this is largely due to its narrow focus. Anomaly-based detection methods often generate high false positives, especially if threshold values are not properly maintained. Although many alerts based on benign activities might occur, such as another organization's WLAN being within the range of the organization's WLANs, these alerts are not truly false positives because they are accurately detecting an unknown WLAN.

Some tuning and customization are required for the wireless IDPS technologies to improve their detection accuracy. The main effort required in the wireless IDPS is in specifying which WLANs, access points, and stations are authorized, and in entering the policy characteristics into the wireless IDPS software. As wireless IDPSs only examine wireless network protocols, not the higher-level protocols (e.g., applications); generally, there are only a few alert types, and consequently not many customizations or tunings are available.

Wireless IDPS sensors provide two types of intrusion prevention capabilities, which are as follows [12]:

- Some sensors can terminate connections through the air, typically by sending messages to the end points telling them to dissociate the current session and then refusing to permit a new connection to be established.
- Another prevention method is for a sensor to instruct a switch on the wired network to block network activity involving a particular device on the basis of the device's media access control address or switch port. However, this technique is only effective for blocking the device's communications on the wired network, not the wireless network.

An important consideration when choosing prevention capabilities is the effect that prevention actions can have

on sensor monitoring. For example, if a sensor is transmitting signals to terminate connections, it may not be
able to perform channel scanning to monitor other communications until it has completed the prevention action.
To mitigate this, some sensors have two radios: one for
monitoring and detection and another for performing prevention actions.

Wireless IDPS limitations. The wireless IDPSs offer great
detection capabilities against authorized activities, but
there are some significant limitations. The use of evasion
techniques is considered as one of the limitations of some
wireless IDPS sensors, particularly against sensor channel
scanning schemes. One example is performing attacks in
very short bursts on channels that are not currently being
monitored. An attacker could also launch attacks on two
channels at the same time. If the sensor detects the first
attack, it cannot detect the second attack unless it scans
away from the channel of the first attack.

Wireless IDPS sensors (physical devices) are also vulnerable to attack. The same DoS attacks (both logical and
physical) that attempt to disrupt WLANs can also disrupt
sensor functions. Additionally, sensors are often particularly vulnerable to physical attacks because they are usually
located in hallways, conference rooms, and other open
areas. Some sensors have antitamper features, which are
designed to look like fire alarms that can reduce the possibility of physically being attacked. All sensors are vulnerable to physical attacks such as jamming, which disrupt
radio-frequency transmissions; there is no defense against
such attacks other than to establish a physical perimeter
around the facility, so that the attackers cannot get close
enough to the WLAN to jam it.

We should mention that the wireless IDPSs cannot
detect certain types of attacks against wireless networks.
An attacker can passively monitor wireless traffic, which
is not detectable by wireless IDPSs. If weak security
methods are used, for example, wired equivalent privacy,
the attacker can then perform offline processing of the

collected traffic to find the encryption key used to provide security for the wireless traffic. With this key, the attacker can decrypt the traffic that was already collected, as well as any other traffic collected from the same WLAN. As the wireless IDPSs cannot detect certain types of attacks against wireless networks, it cannot fully compensate for the use of insecure wireless networking protocols [12].

NBA system. An NBA system examines network traffic or traffic statistics to identify threats that generate unusual traffic flows, such as DDoS attacks, certain forms of malware, and policy violations. In fact, NBA systems have been known by many names, including network behavior anomaly detection software, NBA and response software, and network anomaly detection software. NBA solutions usually have sensors and consoles, and some products also offer management servers (which are sometimes called *analyzers*).

The NBA system has some sensors similar to network-based IDPS sensors, which sniff packets to monitor network activity on one or a few network segments. These sensors may be active or passive and are placed similarly to network-based IDS sensors—at the boundaries between networks, using the same connection methods. Other NBA sensors do not monitor the networks directly, but instead rely on network flow information provided by routers and other networking devices. Flow refers to a particular communication session occurring between hosts. Typical flow data include source and destination IP addresses, source and destination TCP or UDP ports or Internet control message protocol types and codes, the number of packets and number of bytes transmitted in the session, and timestamps for the start and end of the session [12].

NBA system security capabilities. NBA technologies can detect several types of malicious activities. Most NBA system products use primarily anomaly-based detection, along with some stateful protocol analysis techniques. Therefore, most NBA technologies offer no signature-based detection capability, other than allowing administrators to manually set up custom filters that are essentially signatures to detect or stop specific attacks. Most of the types of authorized activities detected by NBA sensors include network-based DoS attacks, network scanning, worms, the use of unexpected application services, and policy violations (e.g., a host attempting to contact another host with which it has no legitimate reason to communicate). The NBA sensors have the ability to determine the origin of an attack. For example, if worms infect a network, NBA sensors can analyze the worm's flows and find the host on the organization's network that first transmitted the worm.

As we had mentioned above, the NBA sensors are anomaly-based detection, so they work primarily by detecting significant deviations from normal behavior; they are most accurate in detecting attacks that generate large amounts of network activity in a short period of time (e.g., DDoS attacks) and attacks that have unusual flow patterns (e.g., worms spreading among hosts). Attacks that are conducted slowly are less accurately detected by NBA sensors, because they cannot detect many attacks until they reach a point where their activity is significantly different from what is expected. The point during the attack at which the NBA software detects it may vary considerably depending on an NBA product's configuration. Configuring sensors to be more sensitive to anomalous activities will cause alerts to be generated more quickly when attacks occur, but more false positives are also likely to be triggered. Conversely, if sensors are configured to be less sensitive to anomalous activity, there will be fewer false positives, but alerts will be generated more slowly, allowing attacks to occur for longer periods of time. False positives can also be caused by benign changes in the environment. For example, if a new service is added to a host and hosts start using it, an NBA sensor is likely to detect this as anomalous behavior.

NBA technologies depend mainly on observing network traffic and developing baselines of expected flows and inventories of host characteristics. NBA products provide automatic update to their base line, which speed up the prevention against unauthorized activities. Administrators might adjust thresholds periodically (e.g., how much additional bandwidth usage should trigger an alert) to take into account changes to the environment.

We mentioned before that the NBA system is anomaly-based, but a few NBA products offer limited signature-based detection capabilities. The supported signatures tend to be very simple, primarily looking for particular values in certain IP, TCP, UDP, or Internet control message protocol header fields. The signature-based capability is most helpful for in-line NBA sensors because they can use the signatures to find and block attacks that a firewall or router might not be capable of blocking. However, even without a signature capability, an in-line NBA sensor might be able to detect and block the attack because of its flow patterns.

NBA technologies overcome other technologies by offering extensive information gathering capabilities, because knowledge of the characteristics of the organization's hosts is needed for most of the NBA product's detection techniques. Additionally, NBA sensors can automatically create and maintain lists of hosts communicating on the organization's monitored networks. They can monitor port usage, perform passive fingerprinting, and use other techniques to gather detailed information on the hosts. Information typically collected for each host includes IP address, the type and version of the operating system, the network services the host provides, and the nature of the host's communications with other hosts. NBA sensors constantly monitor network activity for changes to this information. Additional information on each host's flows is also collected on an ongoing basis.

NBA sensors provide various intrusion prevention capabilities, including sending TCP reset packets to endpoints, performing in-line firewalling, and reconfiguring other network security devices. Most NBA system implementations use prevention capabilities in a limited fashion

or not at all because of false positives; erroneously blocking a single flow could cause major disruptions in network
communications. Prevention capabilities are most often
used for NBA sensors when blocking a specific known
attack, such as a new worm [9,12].

NBA system limitations. NBA technologies overall have great
prevention capabilities against authorized activities, but
also have significant limitations. One of the most important
limitations is the delay in detecting attacks. Some delay is
inherent in anomaly detection methods that are based on
deviations from a baseline, such as increased bandwidth
usage or additional connection attempts. Generally, NBA
technologies often have additional delay caused by their data
sources, especially when they rely on flow data from routers
and other network devices. These data are often transferred
to the NBA system in batches, as frequently as every min-
ute or two, often much less frequently. Therefore, this delay
is considered as a significant limitation of the NBA technologies, because attacks that occur quickly, such as malware
infestations and DoS attacks, may not be detected until they
have already disrupted or damaged systems. To solve the
delay problem, the NBA system can use sensors (software or
hardware component) that do their own packet captures and
analysis instead of relying on flow data from other devices.
However, performing packet captures and analysis is much
more resource-intensive than analyzing flow data. A single
sensor can analyze flow data from many networks or perform direct monitoring (packet captures) itself generally for
a few networks at the most. More sensors may be needed to
do direct monitoring instead of using flow data [10].

Host-based IDPS. Host-based systems monitor the characteristics of a single host and the events occurring within that
host for suspicious activity. Examples of the types of host
characteristics that a host-based IDPS might monitor are
network traffic for that host, system logs, running processes,
application activity, file access and modification, and system

and application configuration changes. Host-based IDPSs are most commonly deployed on critical hosts such as publicly accessible servers and servers containing sensitive information. Additionally, most host-based IDPSs have detection software known as *agents* installed on the hosts of interest. Each agent monitors activity on a single host and may perform prevention actions. Some agents monitor a single specific application service—for example, a Web server program; these agents are also known as *application-based IDPSs*.

Host-based IDPS agents are deployed to critical hosts, such as publicly accessible servers and servers containing sensitive information, although they can be deployed to other types of hosts as well. Some organizations use agents mainly to analyze activity that cannot be monitored by other security controls. For example, network-based IDPS sensors cannot analyze the activity within encrypted network communications, but host-based IDPS agents installed on endpoints can see the unencrypted activity. The network architecture for host-based IDPS deployments is typically simple. Since the agents are deployed on existing hosts on the organization's networks, the components usually communicate over those networks instead of using a separate management network.

To provide more accurate intrusion prevention capabilities, most IDPS agents alter the internal architecture of hosts. This is typically done through a shim, which is a layer of code placed between existing layers of code. A shim intercepts data at a point where that would normally be passed from one piece of code to another. The shim can then analyze the data and determine whether or not that should be allowed or denied. Host-based IDPS agents may use shims for several types of resources, including network traffic, file-system activity, system calls, Windows registry activity, and common applications (e.g., email and Web). Some agents monitor activity without using shims or they analyze artifacts of activity, such as log entries and file modifications. Although these methods are less intrusive to the host, these methods are also generally less effective at detecting attacks and often cannot perform prevention actions.

Host-based IDPS security capabilities. Host-based IDPSs offer good prevention against several types of malicious activities. A combination (signature-based and anomaly-based) is often used by the host-based IDPSs. The signature-based mechanism is used to identify known attacks, whereas the anomaly-based mechanism is used to identify previously unknown attacks.

There are many types of events detected by host-based IDPSs, but this detection is based on the detection techniques that the IDPSs use. Some host-based IDPS products offer several of these detection techniques, while others focus on a few or one. Some specific techniques that are commonly used in host-based IDPSs are as follows [12]:

– *Code analysis*: Agents might analyze attempts to execute malicious code. One technique is executing code in a virtual environment or sandbox to analyze its behavior and compare it to profiles of known good and bad behavior. Another technique is looking for the typical characteristics of stack and heap buffer overflow exploits, such as certain sequences of instructions and attempts to access portions of memory not allocated to the process. System call monitoring is another common technique; it involves knowing which applications and processes should be performing certain actions.

– *Network traffic analysis*: This is often similar to what a network-based IDPS does. Some products can also analyze wireless traffic. Another capability of traffic analysis is that the agent can extract files sent by applications such as email, Web, and peer-to-peer file sharing, which can then be checked for malware.

– *Network traffic filtering*: Agents often include a host-based firewall that can restrict incoming and outgoing traffic for each application on the system, preventing unauthorized access and acceptable use policy violations (e.g., use of inappropriate external services).

- *File-system monitoring*: They can be performed using several different techniques. File integrity checking involves generating cryptographic checksums for critical files and comparing them to reference values to identify which files have been changed. File attribute checking is the process of checking critical files' security attributes, such as ownership and permissions, for changes. Both file integrity and file attribute checking are reactive, detecting attacks only after they have occurred. Some agents have more proactive capabilities, such as monitoring file access attempts, comparing each attempt to an access control policy, and preventing attempts that violate policy.
- *Log analysis*: Some agents can monitor and analyze operating system and application logs to identify malicious activity. These logs may contain information on system operational events, audit records, and application operational events.

As the host-based IDPSs provide extensive knowledge of hosts' characteristics and configurations, an agent can often determine whether an attack would succeed if not stopped. Agents can use this knowledge to select preventive actions and to prioritize alerts.

Like any other IDPS technology, host-based IDPSs often cause false positives and false negatives. However, the accuracy of detection is more challenging for host-based IDPSs because they detect events but do not have knowledge of the context under which the events occurred. For example, a new application may be installed—this could be done by malicious activity or done as part of normal host operations. The event's benign or malicious nature cannot be determined without additional context. Therefore, organizations that would like to use a host-based IDPS are recommended to use a host-based product that use combinations of several detection techniques, which achieve more accurate detection than products that use one or a few techniques. As each technique can monitor different aspects of a host, using more techniques allows agents to have a more complete picture of the events, including additional context.

Considerable tuning and customization are required to achieve better prevention by the host-based IDPSs. For example, many rely on observing host activity and developing profiles of expected behavior. Others need to be configured with detailed policies that define exactly how each application on a host should behave. The policies need to be updated as the host environment changes, so that these changes are taken into account. Some products permit multiple policies to be configured on a host for multiple environments; this is mostly helpful for hosts that function in multiple environments, such as a laptop used both within an organization and from external locations [12].

Host-based IDPS agents provide several intrusion prevention capabilities, based on the detection techniques they use. For example, code analysis techniques can prevent malicious code from being executed, and network traffic analysis techniques can stop incoming traffic from being processed by the host and can prevent malicious files from being placed on the host. Network traffic filtering techniques can block unwanted communications. File-system monitoring can prevent files from being accessed, modified, replaced, or deleted, which could stop installation of malware, including Trojan horses and rootkits, as well as other attacks involving inappropriate file access. Other host-based IDPS detection techniques, such as log analysis, network configuration monitoring, and file integrity, and attribute checking, generally do not support prevention actions because they identify events after they have occurred [11,12].

Host-based IDPS limitations. Host-based IDPSs also have some significant limitations. Although agents generate alerts on a real-time basis for most detection techniques, some techniques are used periodically to identify events that have already had happened. Such techniques might only be applied hourly or even just a few times a day, causing significant delay in identifying certain events. Additionally, many host-based IDPSs are intended to forward their alert data to the management servers on a periodic basis, such as every 15–60 min, to reduce overhead. This can cause delays in initiating response actions, which especially increases the impact of incidents that spread quickly, such as malware infestations. Host-based IDPSs can consume considerable amount of resources on the hosts that they protect, particularly if they use several detection techniques and shims. Host-based IDPSs can also cause conflicts with existing security controls, such as personal firewalls, particularly if those controls also use shims to intercept host activity.

6.3.6 *Integration of Multiple IDPS*

Integration of multiple IDPS technologies and that of different IDPS products offer good prevention mechanism for organizations. We discuss the advantages of integration in detail in the following sections.

Multiple IDPS technologies. We had mentioned earlier that there are four primary types of IDPS technologies: network-based, wireless, NBA, and host-based. Each of these types has different prevention capabilities from other types from unauthorized activities. For example, some of these types can detect attack that other cannot. Therefore, detecting as many attacks as possible will result in a better defense. Accordingly, using multiple types of IDPS technologies can achieve more comprehensive and accurate detection and prevention of malicious activity. For most of the environments, a combination of network-based and host-based IDPSs are needed at a minimum. Wireless IDPSs may also be needed if WLAN security or rogue WLAN detection is a concern. NBA products can also be deployed to achieve stronger detection capabilities for DoS attacks, worms, and other threats that cause anomalous network flows [12].

In fact, some organizations use multiple products of the same IDPS technology type to get more prevention and detection against malicious activities. Because, each product can detect attacks that another product cannot. Therefore, using multiple products can offer more comprehensive and accurate defense. For the organizations that would like to use multiple products of the same IDPS technology type, we recommend them to use one monitoring device for multiple products. One monitoring device makes it easier for analysts to confirm the validity of alerts and identify false positives, and also provides redundancy. Using many monitoring devices will result in a difficult analysis scenario, and will also consume time and resources [2,12].

Integration of different IDPS products. Different IDPS products function completely independently of each other. One of the most important advantages of using different IDPS products is that if one of them is compromised or fails, the other will not be affected, which means that there are other products still giving defense against malicious activity. However, if the products are not integrated, the effectiveness of the entire IDPS implementation may be somewhat limited. Data cannot be shared by the products, and extra effort will be needed to monitor and manage multiple sets of products. IDPS products can be directly or indirectly integrated [2,12].

6.3.7 IDPS Products

All sections above are concerned about the IDPS. Implementation of the above concept will result in IDPS products. There are many IDPS products in the world and each of them has relative advantages over others. Therefore, in this section, we mention some of these products, so that the researchers can know these products, use them, modify the open source of them, and also start a new IPDS product for research [2].

Common enterprise network–based IDPSs
Common enterprise wireless IDPSs
Common enterprise NBA systems
Common enterprise host-based IDPSs

Table 6.1   Network-Based IDPSs

PRODUCT LINE	VENDOR	URL
Attack Mitigator	Top Layer Networks	http://www.toplayer.com/content/products/index.jsp
BBX	DeepNines	http://www.deepnines.com/bbx.php
Bro	Vern Paxson	http://bro-ids.org/
Cisco IPS	Cisco Systems	http://www.cisco.com/en/US/products/hw/vpndevc/index.html
Cyclops	e-Cop.net	http://www.e-cop.net/
DefensePro	Radware, Ltd.	http://www.radware.com/content/products/dp/default.asp
Dragon	Enterasys Networks, Inc.	http://www.enterasys.com/products/ids/
eTrust Intrusion Detection	Computer Associates	http://www3.ca.com/solutions/Product.aspx?ID=163
Juniper Networks IDP	Juniper Networks	https://www.juniper.net/products/intrusion/
IntruShield	Network Associates	http://www.mcafee.com/us/enterprise/products/network_intrusion_prevention/index.html
iPolicy	iPolicy Networks	http://www.ipolicynetworks.com/products/ipf.html
Proventia	Internet Security Systems	http://www.iss.net/products/product_sections/Intrusion_Prevention.html
SecureNet	Intrusion	http://www.intrusion.com/
Sentivist	Check Point Software Technologies	http://www.nfr.com/solutions/sentivist-ips.php
Snort	Sourcefire	http://www.snort.org/
Sourcefire	Sourcefire	http://www.sourcefire.com/products/is.html
StoneGate	StoneSoft Corporation	http://www.stonesoft.com/en/products_and_solutions/products/ips/
Strata Guard	StillSecure	http://www.stillsecure.com/strataguard/index.php
Symantec Network Security	Symantec Corporation	http://www.symantec.com/enterprise/products/index.jsp
UnityOne	TippingPoint Technologies	http://www.tippingpoint.com/products_ips.html

Table 6.2   Wireless IDPSs

PRODUCT LINE	VENDOR	URL
AirDefense	AirDefense	http://www.airdefense.net/products/index.php
AirMagnet	AirMagnet	http://www.airmagnet.com/products/
AiroPeek	WildPackets	http://www.wildpackets.com/products/airopeek/overview
BlueSecure	BlueSocket	http://www.bluesocket.com/products/centralized_intrusion.html
Highwall	Highwall Technologies	http://www.highwalltech.com/products.cfm
Red-Detect	Red-M	http://www.red-m.com/products-and-services/red-detect.html
RFprotect	Network Chemistry	http://networkchemistry.com/products/
SpectraGuard	AirTight Networks	http://www.airtightnetworks.net/products/products_overview.html

Table 6.3   NBA IDPSs

PRODUCT LINE	VENDOR	URL
Arbor Peakflow X	Arbor Networks	http://www.arbornetworks.com/products_x.php
Cisco Guard, Cisco Traffic Anomaly Detector	Cisco Systems	http://www.cisco.com/en/US/products/hw/vpndevc/index.html
GraniteEdge ESP	GraniteEdge Networks	http://www.graniteedgenetworks.com/products
OrcaFlow	Cetacea Networks	http://www.orcaflow.ca/features-overview.php
Profiler	Mazu	http://www.mazunetworks.com/products/index.php
Proventia Network Anomaly Detection System (ADS)	Internet Security Systems	http://www.iss.net/products/Proventia_Network_Anomaly_Detection_System/product_main_page.html
QRadar	Q1 Labs	http://www.q1labs.com/content.php?id=175
StealthWatch	Lancope	http://www.lancope.com/products/

Table 6.4 Host-Based IDPSs

PRODUCT LINE	VENDOR	URL
BlackIce	Internet Security Systems	http://www.iss.net/products/product_sections/ Server_Protection.html http://www.iss.net/products/product_sections/ Desktop_Protection.html
Blink	eEye Digital Security	http://www.eeye.com/html/products/blink/index. html
Cisco Security Agent	Cisco Systems	http://www.cisco.com/en/US/products/sw/ secursw/ps5057/index.html
Deep Security	Third Brigade	http://www.thirdbrigade.com/
DefenseWall HIPS	SoftSphere Technologies	http://www.softsphere.com/programs/
Intrusion SecureHost	Intrusion	http://www.intrusion.com/
McAfee Host Intrusion Prevention	McAfee	http://www.mcafee.com/us/enterprise/products/ host_intrusion_prevention/index.html
Primary Response	Sana Security	http://www.sanasecurity.com/products/pr/index. php
Proventia	Internet Security Systems	http://www.iss.net/products/product_sections/ Server_Protection.html http://www.iss.net/products/product_sections/ Desktop_Protection.html
Intrusion SecureHost	Intrusion	http://www.intrusion.com/
RealSecure	Internet Security Systems	http://www.iss.net/products/product_sections/ Server_Protection.html http://www.iss.net/products/product_sections/ Desktop_Protection.html
SecureIIS Web Server Protection	eEye Digital Security	http://www.eeye.com/html/products/secureiis/ index.html
Symantec Critical System Protection	Symantec	http://www.symantec.com/enterprise/products/ index.jsp

6.3.8 Concluding Remarks

As new network technologies, topologies, and structures are developing, different kinds of attack strategies are also being devised. The hackers are not sitting idle and each day hundreds of experts may try to put their expertise in the negative ways. Hence, different kinds of detection and prevention schemes will be needed to deal with different network scenarios. Constant learning process and setting the defense strategy accordingly could ensure secure functionality of a network.

References

1. H.M. Alsafi, W.M. Abduallah, and A.-S.K. Pathan, IDPS: An integrated intrusion handling model for cloud computing environment, *International Journal of Computing & Information Technology* 4(1), 1–16, January–June 2012.

2. K. Scarfone, and P. Mell, *Guide to Intrusion Detection and Prevention Systems (IDPS)*, National Institute of Standards and Technology Special Publication 800-94, 127 pages, February 2007, csrc.nist.gov/publications/nistpubs/800-94/SP800-94.pdf, last accessed August 11, 2012.

3. A. Abduvaliyev, A.-S.K. Pathan, J. Zhou, R. Roman, and W.-C. Wong, Intrusion detection and prevention in wireless sensor networks, *Wireless Sensor Networks: Current Status and Future Trends*, Eds., Shafiullah Khan, Al-Sakib Khan Pathan, and Nabil Ali Alrajeh, CRC Press, Boca Raton, FL, 2012.

4. J.R. Vacca, *Managing Information Security*, 1st edition, Syngress, Elsevier, Waltham, MA, March 29, 2010.

5. K.K. Frederick, *Network Intrusion Detection Signatures*, Part Three, Security Focus, 2002, http://www.symantec.com/connect/articles/network-intrusion-detection-signatures-part-three, last accessed August 11, 2012.

6. R. Bace, *Intrusion Detection*, New Riders, Indianapolis, IN, 2000.

7. K.K. Frederick, *Network Intrusion Detection Signatures*, Part Five, SecurityFocus, 2002, http://www.symantec.com/connect/articles/network-intrusion-detection-signatures-part-five, last accessed August 11, 2012.

8. A.-S.K. Pathan, M.M. Monowar, and Z.M. Fadlullah, *Building Next-Generation Converged Networks: Theory and Practice*, CRC Press, Boca Raton, FL, 2013.

9. D.J. Marchette, *Computer Intrusion Detection and Network Monitoring: A Statistical Viewpoint (Information Science and Statistics)*, 1st edition, Springer, New York, June 26, 2001.

10. M. Rash, A.D. Orebaugh, G. Clark, B. Pinkard, and J. Babbin, *Intrusion Prevention and Active Response: Deploying Network and Host IPS*, 1st edition, Syngress, Elsevier, Waltham, MA, April 26, 2005.

11. S. Northcutt, L. Zeltser, S. Winters, K. Kent, and R.W. Ritchey, *Inside Network Perimeter Security*, 2nd edition, Sams, Sams Indianapolis, IN, March 14, 2005.

12. M.M.Z.E. Mohammed and A.-S. K. Pathan. Automatic Defense against Zero-day Polymorphic Worms in Communication Networks, ISBN 9781466557277, CRC Press, Taylor & Francis Group, Boca Raton, FL, 2013.

7

COLLECTING ZERO-DAY POLYMORPHIC WORMS USING DOUBLE-HONEYNET

MOHSEN MOHAMED

We have learnt in Chapters 5 and 6 that we need mainly two steps to generate signatures for zero-day polymorphic worms, which are as follows [8]:

- First, we should collect zero-day polymorphic worm samples. To do this, we have to propose any new sample collection method.
- After collecting the samples, we should develop new algorithms to generate signatures for the collected samples.

This chapter will present with examples how the collection process and generation of signatures can be performed. The zero-day polymorphic worm collection method described here (i.e., double-honeynet system) and developed signature generation algorithms: substring extraction algorithm, modified Knuth–Morris–Pratt algorithm, and modified principal component analysis algorithm (MPCA) are worked out by Mohammed et al. in the works like [1–3,8].

This chapter contains two parts. The first part discusses the design of double-honeynet system in detail, while the second part discusses the following:

- Information about the software used to implement the double-honeynet system
- Double-honeynet system configurations using VMware

7.1 Motivation of Double-Honeynet System

Unknown Internet worms pose a major threat to the Internet infrastructure security, and their destruction causes loss of millions

165

of dollars. Security experts manually generate the intrusion detection system signatures by studying the network traces after a new worm has been released. Unfortunately, this job takes a lot of time. We propose a double-honeynet system that could automatically detect unknown worms without any human intervention. In our system, interaction between the two honeynets works by forming a loop, which allows us to collect all instances of polymorphic worm, which enables the system to produce accurate worm signatures. The double-honeynet system is a hybrid system with both network- and host-based mechanisms. This allows us to collect instances of polymorphic worm at the network level and at the host level, which reduces the false positives and false negatives dramatically [8].

7.2 Double-Honeynet Architecture

The purpose of double-honeynet system is to detect unknown (i.e., previously unreported) worms automatically. A key contribution of this system is the ability of distinguishing worm activities from normal activities without any involvement of experts in the field.

Figure 7.1 shows the main components of the double-honeynet system. First, the incoming traffic goes through the local router, which

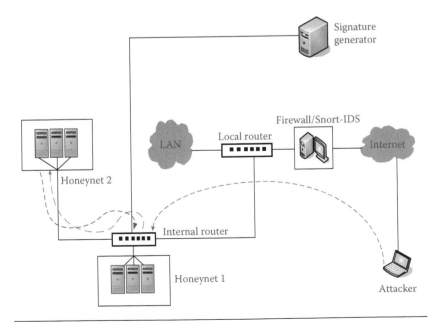

Figure 7.1   Double-honeynet system.

samples the unwanted inbound connections and redirects the samples' connections to Honeynet 1. As the redirected packets pass through the local router, packet capture library is used to capture the packets and then to analyze their payloads to contribute to the signature generation process.

The local router is configured with publicly accessible addresses, which represent wanted services. Connections made to other addresses are considered unwanted and redirected to Honeynet 1 through the internal router. Once Honeynet 1 is compromised, the worm will attempt to make outbound connections to attack another network. The internal router is implemented to separate the double-honeynet from the local area network (LAN). This router intercepts all outbound connections from Honeynet 1 and redirects those to Honeynet 2, which does the same task forming a loop. The looping mechanism allows us to capture different instances of the polymorphic worm as it mutates on each loop iteration.

We stop the loop after a considerable amount of time in order to collect polymorphic worms. More details about how much time is taken to collect such types of attacks are presented in Section 7.4.

Only those packets that make outbound connections are considered as polymorphic worms, and hence the double-honeynet system forwards only the packets that make outbound connections. This policy is in place due to the fact that benign users do not try to make outbound connections if they are faced with nonexisting addresses. In fact, our system collects other malicious activities, which do not intend to propagate themselves but to attack targeted machines only. Such malicious attack is out of our work scope.

When enough instances of worm payloads are collected by Honeynet 1 and Honeynet 2, they are forwarded to the signature generator component, which generates signatures automatically using specific algorithms.

For example in Figure 7.1, if the local router suspects some packet 1 (P_1), packet 2 (P_2), and packet 3 (P_3) to be malicious, it redirects them to the Honeynet 1 through the internal router. Among these three packets, P_1 and P_2 make outbound connections and internal router redirects these outbound connections to Honeynet 2. In Honeynet 2, P_1 and P_2 change their payloads and become P_1' and P_2', respectively (i.e., P_1' and P_2' are the instances of P_1 and P_2). Therefore, in this case, P_1' and P_2'

make outbound connections and the internal router redirects these connections to Honeynet 1. In Honeynet 1, P_1' and P_2' change their payloads and become P_1'' and P_2'', respectively (i.e., P_1'' and P_2'' are also other instances of P_1 and P_2).

Now, P_1 and P_2 are found malicious because of the outbound connections. Therefore, Honeynet 1 forwards P_1, P_1'', P_2, P_2'' to the signature generator for signature generation process. Similarly, Honeynet 2 forwards P_1' and P_2' to the signature generator for signature generation process.

In this scenario, P_3 does not make any outbound connection when it gets to Honeynet 1. Therefore, P_3 is not considered malicious [8].

7.3 Software

The software tools used in the double-honeynet system are introduced below [8].

7.3.1 Honeywall Roo CDROM

The Honeywall Roo CDROM version 1.4 is downloaded from the Honeynet Project and Research Alliance. It provides data capture, control, and analysis capabilities [4,5]. Most importantly, it monitors all traffic that go in and out of the honeynet. Honeywall Roo CDROM runs Snort_inline, an intrusion prevention system based on the intrusion detection system Snort. Snort_inline either drops unwanted packets or modifies them to make them harmless. It records information of all the activities in the honeynet using Sebek. It runs the Sebek server, while the Sebek clients run on the honeypots. The clients then send all captured information to the server. For management and data analysis, it uses the Walleye Web interface. Walleye also works as a maintenance interface, but there is a command-line tool and a dialog menu that can also be used to configure and maintain the Honeywall.

7.3.2 Sebek

Sebek is a data capture tool, which mainly records keystrokes, and also all other types of `sys_read` data [6]. It records and copies all activity on the machine, including changes to files and network communications. The main utility of this tool is to capture network traffic and reassemble the TCP flow. This is in the case of unencrypted data. Encrypted data are another problem, because Sebek can only reassemble it in its encrypted form. Instead of breaking the encryption, Sebek circumvents it by getting the data from the operating system's kernel. Sebek has a client-server architecture. On the client side, it resides entirely in the operating system kernel. Whenever a system call is made, Sebek hijacks it by redirecting it to its own read() call. This way Sebek can capture the data prior to encryption and after decryption.

After capturing the data, the client sends it to the server, which saves it in a database or simply logs the records. The server is normally on the honeywall machine in the case of a honeynet, and it collects data from all the honeypots and puts it all together for analysis.

To prevent detection by intruders, Sebek employs some obfuscation methods. On the client side, it is completely hidden from the user, and therefore, from an intruder on the system as well. This is, however, not enough because the data that are captured have to be sent to the server, thereby exposing itself. Sebek uses a covert channel to communicate with the server. It generates packets to be sent inside Sebek without using the TCP/IP stack and the packets are sent directly to the driver bypassing the raw socket interface. The packets are then invisible to the user, and Sebek modifies the kernel to prevent the user from blocking transition of the packets. Figure 7.2 shows Sebek deployment.

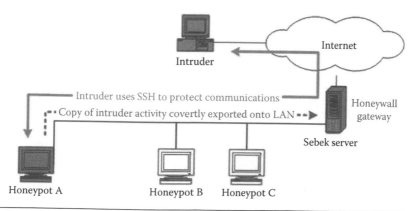

Figure 7.2 Sebek deployment. (Data from *Know Your Enemy: Sebek—A Kernel Based Data Capture Tool*, http://old.honeynet.org/papers/sebek.pdf, 2012.)

In the case of multiple clients, there is a risk of the clients seeing each other's packets. Sebek configures its own raw socket interface on the clients to ignore all incoming Sebek packets. Only the server can receive Sebek packets. Due to its comprehensive log capabilities, it can be used as a tool for forensics data collection. It has a Web interface that can perform data analysis.

7.3.3 Snort_inline

Snort_inline is a modified version of Snort. It is a developed Intrusion Prevention System (IPS) that uses the signatures of existing Intrusion Detection System (IDS) to make decisions on packet that traverse snort_inline. The decisions are usually drop, reject, modify, or allow [7].

7.4 Double-Honeynet System Configurations

In this section, we discuss the double-honeynet system architecture and configuration using VMware [8].

7.4.1 Implementation of Double-Honeynet Architecture

Figure 7.3 shows the architecture of the double-honeynet system, implemented using VMware workstation version 7 on a personal computer with Intel Pentium 4, 3.19-GHz CPU, 8GB RAM, and running on Windows XP 64-bit. The operating system of that personal computer is referred to as the *host operating system* in Figure 7.3. The host machine was connected to our home router and it accessed the Internet through it.

We used virtual machine to deploy the double-honeynet system due to the lack of resources and to keep the establishment cost low. One personal computer was used and VMware workstation was installed on it. The VMware workstation is a software package that gives its users the opportunity to create virtual machines that constitute virtual networks interconnected with each other. Thus, we created the double-honeynet system as a virtual network seen from the outside world as an independent network. Attackers could locate the honeypot and attack it. The honeypot was transparently connected to the Internet through the honeywall, which in turn intercepted all outbound and inbound traffic. Therefore, malicious traffic targeting the honeypot (inbound) or malicious traffic generated by

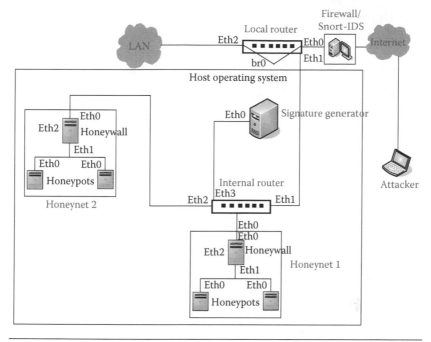

Figure 7.3   Double-honeynet architecture.

the compromised honeypot (outbound) were available to us from the honeywall for further analysis and investigation. As we mentioned in Section 7.2, Honeynet 1 and Honeynet 2 were configured to deliver unlimited outbound connections. The *internal router* was used to protect our local network by redirecting all outbound connections from Honeynet 1 to Honeynet 2 and vice versa.

7.4.2 Double-Honeynet Configurations

Our double-honeynet system contains six components: local router, internal router, LAN, Honeynet 1, Honeynet 2, and signature generator. The subnet mask for each subnet (whether local router, internal router, LAN, Honeynet 1, Honeynet 2, and signature generator) is consequently 255.255.255.0. Sections 7.4.2.1 through 7.4.2.6 discuss the configurations of each component.

> *Local router configuration.* As we mentioned in Section 7.2, the local router's function is to pass unwanted traffic to the Honeynet 1 through the internal router. For example, if the

IP address space of our LAN is 212.0.50.0/24, with one public Web server, the server's IP address is 212.0.50.19. If an
attacker outside the network launches a worm attack against
212.0.50.0/24, the worm scans the IP address space of victims. It is highly probable that an unused IP address, for
example, 212.0.50.10 will be attempted before 212.0.50.19.
Therefore, the local router will redirect the packet to
Honeynet 1 through the internal router. After the worm
compromises the Honeynet 1, the worm will try to make
an outbound connection to harm another network. We configured the internal router to protect the LAN from worms'
outbound connections. The internal router intercepts all outbound connections from Honeynet 1 and redirects them to
Honeynet 2, which performs the same task being done by
the Honeynet 1, forming loop connections. Below are the
details of the local router machine properties and IP-tables
configuration.

Machine Properties
- *Operating system*: Ubuntu Linux 9.10
- *Number of network cards*:
    - Three network cards (Eth0, Eth1, and Eth2)
        - Eth0 and Eth2 are bridged LAN port
        - The function of Eth1 is to connect the local router
          with Honeynet 1 through the internal router
- *IP addresses*:
    - Eth1: 192.168.50.20
- Prior to the IP-tables setting, we enabled IP forwarding
  in the local router
    - Edit/etc/sysctl.conf file as follows:
        - `Net.ipv4.ip _ frowrd =1`
- *IP-tables configuration*:
  The settings of the network address translator in the ker-
  nel using IP-tables are as follows:
    - Do not translate packets going to the real public server:
        - `# Iptables -t nat -A PREROUTING`
          `-m physdev --physdev-in eth0 -d`
          `212.0.50.19 -j RETURN`

- Translate all other packets going to the public LAN to the internal router:
  - # Iptables -t nat -A PREROUTING -m physdev --physdev-in eth0 -d 212.0.50.0/24 -j DNAT --to 192.168.50.22

Internal router configuration. Again, as mentioned in Section 7.2, the internal router's function is to protect the LAN from worms' outbound connections and to redirect the outbound connections from Honeynet 1 to Honeynet 2 and vice versa. Let us investigate more about the internal router machine properties and IP-tables configuration in the following texts.

Machine Properties
- *Operating system*: Ubuntu Linux 9.10
- *Number of network cards*:
  - Four network cards (Eth0, Eth1, Eth2, and Eth3)
    - The function of Eth0 is to connect the internal router to the Honeynet 1 clients
    - The function of Eth1 is to connect the internal router with the local router
    - The function of Eth2 is to connect the internal router to Honeynet 2 clients
    - The function of Eth3 is to connect the internal router with the signature generator
- *IP addresses*:
  - Eth0: 192.168.51.20
  - Eth1: 192.168.50.22
  - Eth2: 192.168.58.20
  - Eth3: 192.168.55.20
- Before we set the IP-tables rules, we enable the IP forwarding in the internal router:
  - Edit/etc/sysctl.conf file as follows:
    - Net.ipv4.ip _ frowrd =1
- *IP-tables configuration*:
  The settings of the network address translator in the kernel using IP-tables are as follows:
  - Translate packets coming in from Eth1 to the Honeynet 1

```
# Iptables -t nat -A PREROUTING -i
    eth1 -j DNAT --to 192.168.51.22
```
- From Honeynet 1, do not translate packets to the signature generator
```
# Iptables -t nat -A PREROUTING -i eth0 -s
    192.168.51.22 -d 192.168.55.22 -j RETURN
```
- From Honeynet 1, translate all other packet to Honeynet 2
```
# Iptables -t nat -A PREROUTING -i
    eth0 -j DNAT --to 192.168.58.22
```
- From Honeynet 2, do not translate packets to the signature generator
```
# Iptables -t nat -A PREROUTING -i eth0 -s
    192.168.58.22 -d 192.168.55.22 -j RETURN
```
- From Honeynet 2, translate all other packets to Honeynet 1
```
# Iptables -t nat -A PREROUTING -i eth0
    -j DNAT --to 192.168.51.22
```

LAN configuration. As described in subsection 7.4.2.1, we have one public Web server in our LAN with this IP address: 212.0.50.19. Below are the details of the public Web server machine properties.

Machine Properties
- *Operating system*: Ubuntu Linux 9.10
- *Number of network cards:*
- One network card: Eth0
- *IP address*:
  Eth0: 212.0.50.19

Honeynet 1 configuration. As shown in Figure 7.3, Honeynet 1 contains honeywall and two honeypots. The main function of the Honeynet 1 is to capture instances of polymorphic worms. Below are the details of the honeywall machine properties and configuration.

Machine Properties
- *Number of network cards*:
  - Three network cards (Eth0, Eth1, and Eth2)
    - The function of Eth0 is to connect Honeynet 1 with Honeynet 2 through the internal router

- The function of Eth1 is to connect Honeynet 1 with its clients (honeypots)
- Eth2 is used for management interface
- *IP addresses*:
  - Eth0: 192.168.51.22
  - Eth1: 192.168.52.20
  - Eth2: 192.168.40.7
- *Honeywall configurations*
  - *Honeynet public IP addresses*
    Here, we type the external IP addresses for the honeypots. These IP addresses are the attackers:
    IP addresses: 192.168.52.22; 192.168.52.23
  - *Honeynet network*
    Here, we type the honeynet network in classless interdomain routing (CIDR) notation:
    Honeynet network CIDR: 192.168.52.0/24
  - *Broadcast address of the honeynet*: 192.168.52.255
  - *Management interface:*
    The third interface will be used for remote management. This interface helps us to remotely manage the honeywall through secure shell (SSH) and Walleye Web interfaced. We use Eth2 for the management interface
    IP address of the management interface: 192.168.40.7
    Network mask of the management interface: 255.255.255.0
    Default gateway for the management interface: 198.168.40.1
    DNS server IP for honeywall gateway: 192.168.40.2
    SSH listening port: 22
    Space delimited list of TCP ports allowed into the management interface: 22 443
    Space delimited list of IP addresses that can access the management interface: 192.168.40.0/24
  - *Firewall restrictions:*
    The double-honeynet configured to perform unlimited outbound connections as mentioned in (7.2) above
  - *Configure Sebek variables*
    Sebek is a data capture tool designed to capture the attackers' activities on a honeypot. It has two components. The first is a client that runs on the honeypots;

its purpose is to capture all of the attackers' activities (keystrokes, file uploads, and passwords), and then to covertly send the data to the server. The second component is the server, which collects the data from the honeypots. The server normally runs on the honeywall gateway.

Destination IP address of the Sebek packets: 192.268.52.20

Destination UDP port of the Sebek packets: 1101

– *Honeypots configuration*

The following are the details of the honeypots machines properties and configuration:

– *Honeypot 1*

Machine properties:

Operating system: Windows XP

Number of network cards:

We use only one network card: Eth0

IP address:

Eth0: 192.168.52.22

– *Honeypot 2*

Machine properties:

Operating System: Ubuntu Linux 9.10

Number of network cards:

We use one network card: Eth0

IP address:

Eth0: 192.168.52.23

Honeynet 2 configuration. Honeynet 2 contains honeywall and two honeypots. The function of Honeynet 2 is to capture instances of polymorphic worms. The following are the details of the honeywall machine properties and configuration:

Machine Properties

• *Number of network cards*:

– Three network cards (Eth0, Eth1, and Eth2)

– The function of Eth0 is to connect Honeynet 2 with Honeynet 2 through the internal router

– The function of Eth1 is to connect Honeynet 2 with its clients (honeypots)

– Eth2 is used for management interface

- *IP addresses*:
  - Eth0: 192.168.58.22
  - Eth1: 192.168.59.20
  - Eth2: 192.168.40.8
- *Honeywall configuration*
  - *Honeynet public IP addresses*

    In the following, we type the external IP addresses for the honeypots. These IP addresses are the attackers:

    IP addresses: 192.168.59.22; 192.168.59.23
  - *Honeynet network*

    Here, we type the honeynet network in CIDR notation:

    Honeynet network CIDR: 192.168.59.0/24
  - *Broadcast address of the honeynet*: 192.168.59.255
  - *Management interface:*

    The third interface will be used for remote management. This interface helps us to remotely manage the honeywall through SSH and Walleye Web interfaced. We use Eth2 for the management interface.

    IP address of the management interface: 192.168.40.8

    Network mask of the management interface: 255.255.255.0

    Default gateway for the management interface: 198.168.40.1

    DNS server IP for honeywall gateway: 192.168.40.2

    SSH listening port: 22

    Space delimited list of TCP ports allowed into the management interface: 22 443

    Space delimited list of IP addresses that can access the management interface: 192.168.40.0/24
  - *Firewall restrictions:*

    The double-honeynet configured to perform unlimited outbound connections as mentioned in (7.2) above
  - *Configure Sebek variables*

    Destination IP address of the Sebek packets: 192.68.59.20

    Destination UDP port of the Sebek packets: 1101

– *Honeypots configuration*
The following are the details of the honeypots machines properties:

– *Honeypot 1*
Machine properties:
Operating system: Windows XP
Number of network cards. We use one network card: Eth0
IP address: 192.168.59.22

– *Honeypot 2*
Machine properties:
Operating system: Ubuntu Linux 9.10
Number of network cards: We use one network card: Eth0
IP address: 192.168.59.23

Signature generator configuration. The function of the signature generator is to generate signatures for polymorphic worms samples.

Machine Properties

- *Operating system*: Ubuntu Linux 9.10
- *Number of network cards*:
  One network card: Eth0
- *IP address*:
  Eth0: 192.168.55.22

7.5 Summary

This chapter discussed two parts. In the first part, we gave full details of the double-honeynet system. In the second part, we gave a brief introduction about the software used to implement the double-honeynet system and double-honeynet configurations using VMware.

References

1. M.M.Z.E. Mohammed, H.A. Chan, N. Ventura, M. Hashim, and I. Amin, A modified Knuth-Morris-Pratt algorithm for zero-day polymorphic worms detection, *Proceedings of the International Conference on Security & Management*, 2 Vols, CSREA Press, Las Vegas, NV, pp. 652–657, July 13–16, 2009.

2. M.M.Z.E. Mohammed, and H.A. Chan, Honeycyber: Automated signature generation for zero-day polymorphic worms, *Proceedings of the IEEE Military Communications Conference*, San Diego, CA, pp. 1–6, November 17–19, 2008.
3. M.Z.E.M. Mohssen, H.A. Chan, N. Ventura, M. Hashim, and I. Amin, Accurate signature generation for polymorphic worms using principal component analysis, *Proceedings of the IEEE GLOBECOM Workshop on Web and Pervasive Security*, Miami, FL, pp. 1555–1560, December 6–10, 2010.
4. *Know Your Enemy: Honeywall CDROM Roo*, https://projects.honeynet.org/honeywall/, last accessed August 18, 2012.
5. The Honeynet Project. *Roo CDROM User's Manual*, http://old.honeynet.org/tools/cdrom/roo/manual/index.html, last accessed August 18, 2012.
6. *Know Your Enemy: Sebek—A Kernel Based Data Capture Tool*, http://old.honeynet.org/papers/sebek.pdf, last accessed August 18, 2012.
7. *Snort—The de facto standard for intrusion detection/prevention*, http://www.snort.org, last accessed August 18, 2012.
8. M.M.Z.E. Mohammed and A.-S. K. Pathan. Automatic Defense against Zero-day Polymorphic Worms in Communication Networks, ISBN 9781466557277, CRC Press, Taylor & Francis Group, Boca Raton, FL, 2013.

Index

Note: Locator followed by '*f*' and '*t*' denotes figure and table in the text

Printed and bound by CPI Group (UK) Ltd, Croydon, CR0 4YY

24/10/2024

01778283-0004